CANOE INDIANS
OF
DOWN EAST MAINE

CANOE INDIANS

OF

DOWN EAST MAINE

WILLIAM A. HAVILAND

THE
History
PRESS

Published by The History Press
Charleston, SC 29403
www.historypress.net

Front cover top, left to right: John. M. Roberts, Anita de L. Haviland, Abbe Museum
Bottom: Abbe Museum
Back cover top: Abbe Museum
Bottom: Library and Archives of Canada

First published 2012
Second printing 2015

ISBN 978.1.54020.718.0

Library of Congress Cataloging-in-Publication Data

Haviland, William A.
Canoe indians of the down east coast / William A. Haviland.
p. cm.
Includes bibliographical references and index.
ISBN 978-1-60949-665-4
1. Indians of North America--Maine--History. 2. Indians of North America--Maine--
Social life and customs. 3. Abenaki Indians--History. 4. Abenaki Indians--Social life and
customs. I. Title.
E78.M2H39 2012
974.1004'97--dc23
2012026055

To All the Wabanaki People
The Real Heroes of This Story

Contents

Acknowledgements

My interest in the coastal Indians of Maine began as a child, back in the 1930s on Deer Isle. Each summer, we would visit the "Indian Camp," a large canvas tent full of baskets, toy birch-bark canoes and other items designed to appeal to the tastes of "rusticators," as the summer people were called. The proprietor was Lawrence Mitchell, member of a Penobscot family descended from Etchemin ancestors. It was this early interest that led me to anthropology.

Though I did not know it at the time, this book had its beginning in 1956, when I did a senior honor's paper for my bachelor's degree in anthropology at the University of Pennsylvania. As it happened, the department there was founded by Frank G. Speck, who authored a number of important works on the Penobscot Indians. Although he was gone by the time I came along, two of his students—Loren Eiseley and A. Irving Hallowell—were on the faculty.

Two years after the BA, I did an extended master's thesis on Maine archaeology. It was based strictly on library research, and I read just about everything ever written on the subject up to then. I intended to pursue this interest, but in a meeting with Wendell Hadlock, one of the pioneers of Maine archaeology (and another of Speck's students), I was told that "a person could starve going into Maine archaeology." At the same time, I became involved in Maya archaeology, diverting me from my early interest. Nevertheless, I'm sure my early focus on Maine's Indians, past and present, has influenced my more recent thinking.

I returned to my early interest in 2003, by which time much more had been learned about Maine's Indians. In that year, I self-published a small book called *Deer Isle's Original People*, which provided something of a template for this book. An earlier book, *The Original Vermonters*, which I co-authored with Marjory Power, also played a role in this book. I rewrote a section that I had written on Abenaki shamans, adapting it as needed to apply to the Etchemins of the coast. Finally, all of the work I did for my last book, *At the Place of the Lobsters and Crabs*, has proven useful here as well.

Many people have contributed to the thinking that has gone into this book, going all the way back to Wendell Hadlock. Others with whom I have had the good fortune to discuss Maine Indians, past and present, include Douglas Byers, John Crock, Steve Cox, Mark Hedden, Doug Kellogg, Charles Paquin, Jim Petersen, Harold Prins and Bunny McBride, David Sanger, Nick Smith, Dean Snow and Art Spiess. I have learned from you all.

I wish, also, to acknowledge a debt to my Wabanaki friends and acquaintances for help and stimulation over the years. Besides the late Lawrence Mitchell, they are Penobscots James Eric Francis Sr., John Bear Mitchell, Charles Shay and Passamaquoddy Donald Soctomah. To you all, *woliwan*—thank you, for all you have shared with me.

I am grateful as well for the encouragement I have received from the staff at the Abbe Museum, particularly CEO Cinnamon Caitlin-Legutko, curator of collections Julia Clark and curator of education Raney Bench. To Julia, thanks as well for providing several illustrations for this book. Support has come as well from the Deer Isle-Stonington Historical Society, especially past and present presidents Paul Stubing and Tinker Crouch, not to mention archivist Connie Wiberg.

My gratitude goes to several people who provided illustrative material: Barbara McDade, director of the Bangor Public Library; Laurent J. Beauregard of the Tarratine Club; Dan Belknap at the University of Maine; Steve Cox; John Crock; Dani Fazio of the Maine Historical Society; Ann Flewelling; Bill Harvey of Harvey Severance in Burlington, Vermont; Mark Hedden; Roger Hooke; the late Jim Peterson; Harold Prins; Bunny McBride; John Roberts; and Brian Robinson. All are credited with the appropriate illustration. Thanks, too, to Art Spiess, who provided me with information on the Dresden Falls site, as well as some of the artifact illustrations in Chapter 1. Julia Clark at the Abbe Museum granted permission for the use of the table included in Chapter 2. Finally, my heartfelt thanks go to Charles Norman Shay for the privilege of photographing him at his home on Indian Island.

ACKNOWLEDGEMENTS

Thanks to Whitney Tarella at The History Press, who provided the idea for this book and essential guidance as it took shape, and production editor Darcy Mahan, who completed the process.

And special thanks to my wife, Anita de Laguna Haviland, who did the word processing, offered important editorial advice and handled e-mail and the difficult job of securing images and permissions, all while putting up with my various requests and preoccupations. Even more important, though, has been her unfailing love and support.

Introduction

In 1604, when the Sieur de Mons and his lieutenant, Samuel de Champlain, stepped ashore on Saint Croix Island, they were far from the first people to do so. For thousands of years, others had lived, loved and labored on this and other islands, as well as on the mainland. Indeed, had it not been for aid provided by the natives of the region, perhaps none of the French would have survived that first difficult winter on the island. It was also two local natives who served as guides as Champlain explored the coast as far west as the Kennebec River in the summer of 1604.

Who were these natives with whom Champlain and his fellow Frenchmen interacted? Unfortunately, there has been a great deal of confusion over who lived where along the shores of Maine and New Brunswick. One source of this confusion stems from the use of linguistic labels in early French accounts, though regional terms were used by the English. So it was that people known to the English as Pemaquids, Penobscots, Machias, Passamaquoddies and Saint John's Indians were known collectively to the French as Etchemins. To further complicate matters, the French began to use other labels, such as when they applied the Mi'kmaq word *Maliseet* to Etchemins. Then, too, the upsets caused by conflicts, massive die-offs from disease and the loss of lands following the influx of Europeans caused all sorts of dislocations and regroupings on the part of the survivors.

Despite these problems, a clear picture exists of who was who along the shores of the Gulf of Maine. Living along the coast between the Kennebec and Saint John Rivers were the Etchemins, whose name for themselves

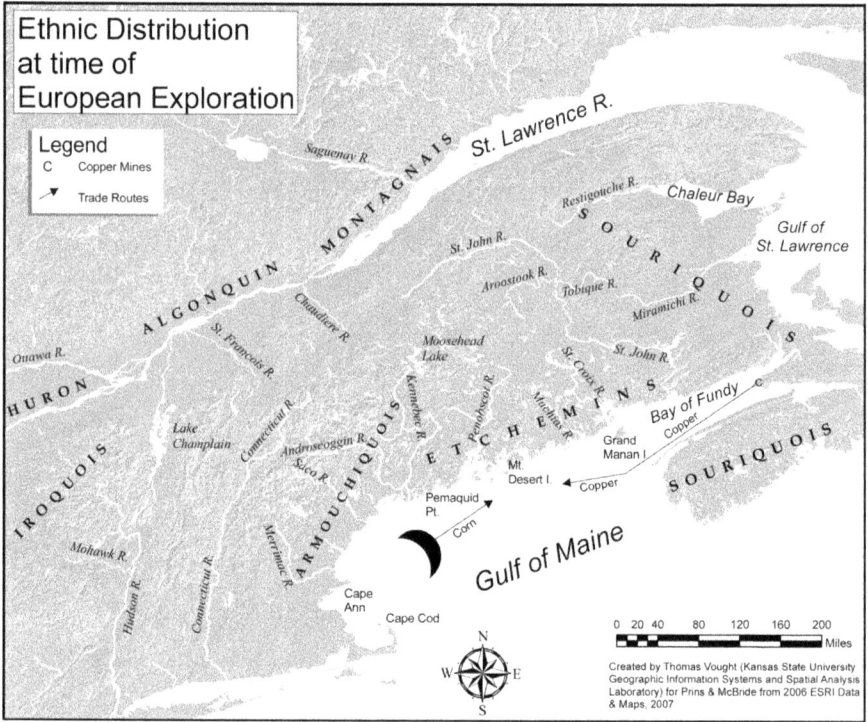

Ethnic distribution at the time of European Exploration. *Prins and McBride 2007: 51. Courtesy Harald E.L. Prins.*

A depiction of Armouchiquois and Montagnais Indians from Champlain's 1612 map of New France. The Montagnais (now called Innu), who lived north of the St. Lawrence River, are the ones who introduced the term Abenaki to the French.

means "real people," as opposed to animals, monsters and other people seen as less than truly human. Their homeland they called *Ketakamigwa*, meaning "the big land on the sea coast." West of them lived a people whom the French called *Armouchiquois*, from a Mi'kmaq word meaning "dog people," not intended as a compliment. Included were groups living as far south as Cape Cod, among them the *Abenakis* ("dawn land people"), whose homeland extended from the Kennebec to the Merrimack River and west to Lake Champlain. Their name for themselves was *Alnambak*, meaning "real people"; the name Abenaki is a corruption of what Indians living in Quebec called them. French settlers in Quebec began to use the name in 1628 at a time when their food resources were running dangerously low. In the nick of time, local Indians arrived with news of a people to the southeast—the direction of the winter sunrise—who were willing to furnish aid.

North and east of the Etchemins lived people the French called *Souriquois*, known from the late 1600s as *Mi'kmaqs* (meaning "kin friends"). Their original name for themselves was *L'nu'k* meaning (guess what?) "humans" or "people." The name Souriquois may derive from the Shediak River, called the Souricoua by the early French. This was part of an important travel route between the Gulf of St. Lawrence and the Bay of Fundy that ran right through the middle of Souriquois country.

All these people spoke closely related languages, variants of Eastern Algonquian, and had long traded with one another. Animal hides and copper from mines in the Minas Basin of Nova Scotia were exchanged for corn and beans grown by the Abenakis. This peaceful exchange was upset in the sixteenth century with the arrival of the French in Mi'kmaq country. Redirecting their trade to these newcomers (called *wenuj*, meaning "who is that?"), the Mi'kmaqs gained access to guns and sailing vessels, allowing them to raid their neighbors along the coast for the things that they had earlier obtained through trade. Allied with them in this raiding were the Etchemins living east of the Narraguagas River (which flows through Cherryfield), who are known today as *Passamaquoddies* ("people of the pollock plenty place") and *Maliseets* ("funny talkers"). Collectively, these people were called *Tarrentines* ("traders") by the English.

To defend themselves against these raiders from Down East, the western Etchemins entered into an alliance with those Abenakis living between the Kennebec and Mousam Rivers. Known as the *Mawooshen* Confederacy, the name means "band of people walking or acting together." The name "Mousam" is a corruption of Mawooshen. The confederacy was headed by a grand chief named Bashaba, whose headquarters was up the Penobscot

Already accomplished mariners, Mi'kmaqs quickly mastered the use of European shallops, such as this one. So it was that, in 1602, the English captain Bartholomew Gosnold encountered Mi'kmaq traders sailing in a shallop off Cape Neddick in southern Maine. Drawing by Duane A. Cline. *Courtesy Bunny McBride.*

River at the mouth of the Kenduskeag Stream. As was the custom when referring to people or things preeminent of their kind, he was often referred to as "The Bashaba," a practice that has confused many historians.

Disaster befell the Mawooshen Confederacy in 1615, when Mi'kmaq raiders managed to kill Bashaba. On top of this came the Great Dying, one of several epidemics that swept through native populations in the Americas. Of European origin, this epidemic killed off up to 90 percent of coastal populations. To replenish their numbers, the local Etchemins encouraged their surviving Abenaki allies, who were under pressure from the growth of English colonies to the south, to join their communities. It is these Abenaki and Echemin descendants of the old Mawooshen Confederacy who became known as *Penobscots*. Eventually, the Abenaki language became dominant among them, although some Etchemin words still persist today. Among the Passamaquoddy and Maliseet, by contrast, modern versions of the old Etchemin language are still spoken.

By 1700, in the face of continual pressures from the English, the Penobscots joined with other Abenakis, as well as their former adversaries Down East, to form the *Wabanaki* ("dawn land") Confederacy. On a grander scale, it represented a revival of the old Mawooshen idea. Still today, these people of northern New England and Canada's Atlantic Provinces are collectively known as Wabanakis.

The superiority of canoe transport over all other modes is apparent from this map of waterways in the state of Maine (The network of rivers, lakes and streams continues eastward into New Brunswick.) The waterways not only made canoe travel possible but also, except when they were iced over, impeded overland travel. *Courtesy David Cook and Ann Flewelling.*

In addition to speaking their own version of the Eastern Algonquian language, each of the Wabanaki nations maintained its own distinct culture. The Etchemins and Mi'kmaqs, for example, relied on hunting, fishing and the gathering of shellfish and wild plants for their subsistence. The Abenakis engaged in these activities, too, but also grew corn, beans and squash. But all of these groups understood one another's language, traded with one another and even intermarried. Thus, despite particular differences, they had much in common as well. Perhaps the most obvious is their reliance on canoe transportation. Except when ice prevented it, most of their travel was by canoe over the extensive network of lakes, rivers and streams of

Birch-bark canoes like this one were so well suited for the waterways of the Down East coast that they remained in use throughout the nineteenth century, when they were largely replaced by canvas. *Courtesy Abbe Museum.*

the Northeast. Etchemin and Mi'kmaq families, in particular, spent a great deal of time in their canoes, traveling from one favorite campsite to another, coming together periodically at traditional gathering places to trade and socialize—hence their depiction as "Canoe Indians." Even the Gulf of Maine itself provided opportunities, as Etchemins made trips to offshore islands like Monhegan and Matinicus. Both they and the Mi'kmaqs traveled to and from Nova Scotia across the open waters of the Bay of Fundy. Truly, these people were skilled mariners.

In the following pages, we will focus our attention on the Etchemins in particular, looking first at their background and then their way of life and how they have coped over the past four hundred years.

Chapter 1

The Archaeological Background

A lthough there is general agreement that the ancestors of the historic Etchemins have been living along the coast for something like 3,000 years, not all scholars agree that people living here before that are ancestral to more recent populations. Some think that there was a population replacement about 3,800 years ago, but many others are skeptical. I belong to the latter group, and today's Wabanakis also see themselves as having been in place since the beginning. But more about this later.

Written records pertaining to the Gulf of Maine's original inhabitants are almost nonexistent before 1604, so to learn about earlier history, we must turn to archaeology for information. Along the coast, numerous shell middens were formed as refuse was discarded by people in the course of their daily activities. Although these middens have suffered in varying degrees from the effects of erosion caused by rising sea levels, until the past few decades, they were little disturbed by development or the activities of relic collectors. Therefore, they preserve a record of people's past activities over the many millennia before the advent of written records. This record is retrievable, however, only through careful and meticulous excavation, usually by professionally trained archaeologists. The good news is that many sites along the coast, both on islands and the nearby mainland, have been professionally excavated; the bad news is that many hitherto untouched sites have been disturbed in recent decades by untrained diggers, with a consequent loss of irreplaceable information.

In addition to the shell middens, archaeologists have also investigated a number of interior sites, often near the falls of rivers and streams where people fished and portaged their canoes or at other good fishing spots. Though it may seem that archaeologists are merely digging up things, what they are really digging up is information. That information comes not from recovered potsherds, spear points and other artifacts by themselves, but rather from the way these objects are associated with one another, as well as with other things such as charcoal, fire-cracked rock, plant, fish and animal remains and so forth. Once taken out of context, objects by themselves tell us next to nothing. Thus, to dig around in archaeological sites looking for relics destroys them, and the information they contain, as effectively as if they were bulldozed into oblivion.

PALEO-INDIANS

Archaeology has revealed that the first people to arrive in the Northeast did so at a time of far-reaching environmental change. Up until eighteen thousand years ago, the region was buried beneath ice more than a mile thick that extended east to the edge of the continental shelf and as far south as Long Island Sound. But then, in response to climatic warming, this glacier began to melt away, receding northward over the next several millennia. By twelve thousand years ago, the edge of the ice had receded north of the Saint Lawrence River, allowing vegetation to spread into the region. First came plants at home in tundra-like conditions, but as warming continued, plant communities continued to change; gradually, trees such as spruce and fir began to take hold, augmented by birch, alder and some other hardwood species over time.

As the glaciers continued to melt, huge amounts of water were released into the seas. Meanwhile, the land, which had been greatly depressed by the weight of the ice, began to rebound (much as the surface of a sponge will rebound if a weight is removed from it). There was, however, a lag between removal of the weight and uplift of the land; hence, the waters rose faster than the land at first. As a consequence, by about twelve thousand years ago, salt water had flooded the coastal lowlands and river valleys, extending as far as one hundred kilometers inland from the present coastline. In the Penobscot and Kennebec Valleys, for example, seawater reached as far north as Medway and Bingham, respectively. In short, anything below about 120 meters elevation today was under water!

Because the rate of crustal uplift ultimately caught up with and surpassed the rate of sea level rise, by ten thousand years ago, water levels had fallen as

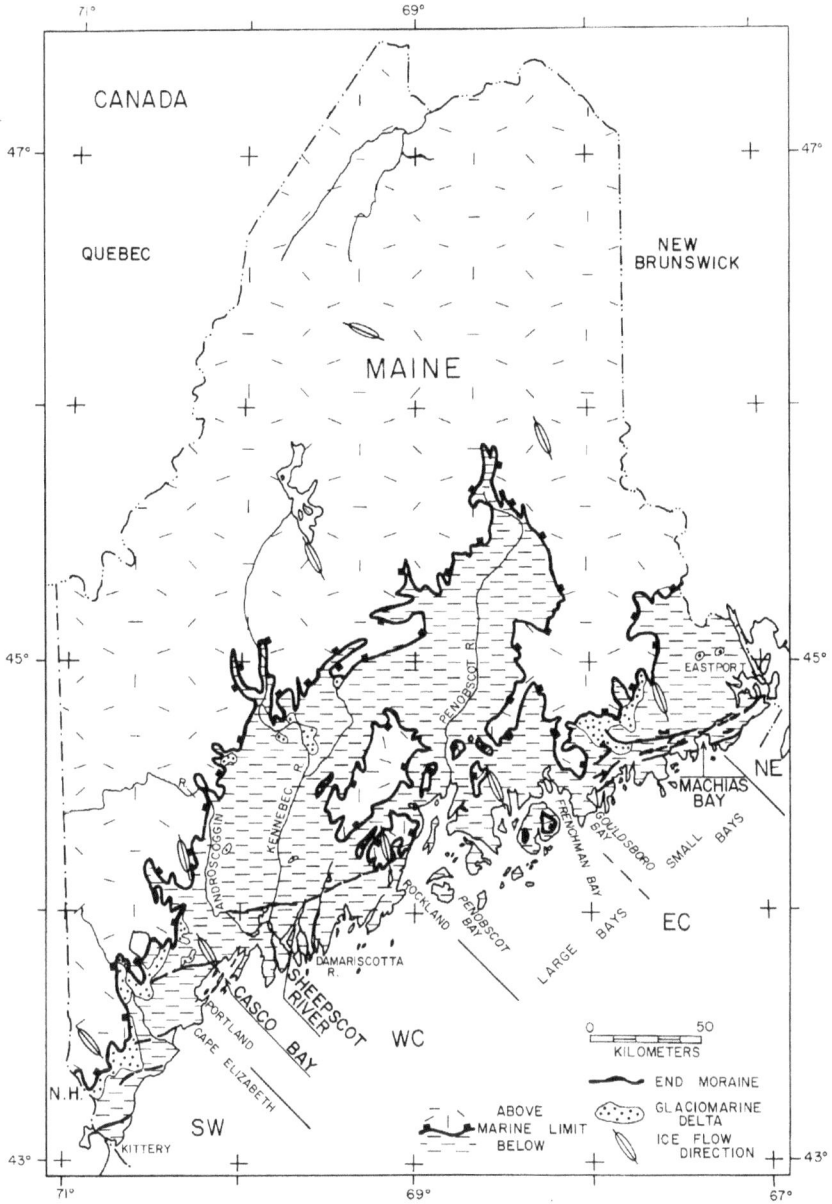

This map shows the extent of flooding in Maine when sea levels (shown in dark) were at their height some twelve thousand years ago. *Courtesy Dan Belknap.*

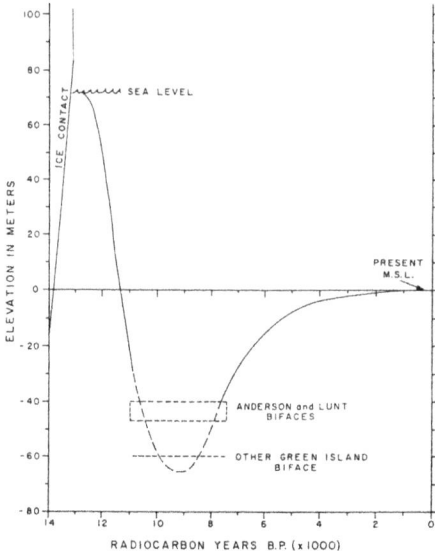

This graph shows how sea levels have risen and fallen in the Gulf of Maine over the past fourteen thousand years. The "Anderson biface" is illustrated below. *Courtesy of the late James Petersen.*

many as sixty meters below where they are today. This exposed a great deal of land and put shorelines up to twenty kilometers southeast of their present location. At that point, rates of sea-level rise and crustal uplift again reversed, and salt water began once again to drown low-lying areas. Although this rise was rapid at first, it decreased over time until, fairly recently, it began to increase again.

During this period of striking environmental change, evidently by 11,500 years ago, the first people began to drift into Maine and Canada's Maritime Provinces. This happened probably not as a deliberate migration, but rather gradually, as population growth in regions to the south nudged people into empty areas in the north. At the same time, populations adapted to particular environments would have been pulled northward in response to climatic warming and the consequent shift of vegetation zones. These first people, whom archaeologists call Paleo-Indians, were hunters of big game, including caribou, mammoths and mastodons. All were available here 11,000 years ago. They hunted smaller animals, as well, including arctic fox and beaver.

On the coast, they may also have preyed on the bearded seals and walrus that were present. They, no doubt, had some kind of watercraft, as evidence from Vermont suggests that Paleo-Indians were exploiting the resources of the saltwater sea that filled the Champlain Basin when sea levels were at their height. And, like all known hunting people, they no doubt gathered both edible and medicinal plants as these were seasonally available.

The Archaeological Background

Although a number of Paleo-Indian sites have been investigated in Maine and the Canadian Maritimes, not to mention New Hampshire, Vermont and Massachusetts, none has been found on the immediate coast. However, isolated Paleo-Indian spear points have been picked up at such places as Arrowsic, Boothbay and Mount Desert. These so-called fluted points are highly distinctive; the fluting was accomplished by removing, from the base, long flakes running about halfway up each face of the point. This thinned area could be inserted easily into the notched end of a wooden shaft for secure hafting. The design was perfectly suited for easy penetration of the hide and flesh of animals both large and small.

An assortment of Paleo-Indian tools from Maine. In the top row and middle row left are the distinctive fluted points. The other tools were for cutting, scraping and woodworking. *Courtesy Arthur Spiess, Maine Historic Preservation Commission.*

Besides these spear points, Paleo-Indian sites include a variety of sharp stone knives and flakes for cutting meat, scrapers for processing hides into clothing, bedding and bags and gravers and scrapers for working both wood and bone. Although they used stone from sources in Maine, such as rhyolite (silica-rich stone of volcanic origin) from Mount Kineo on Moosehead Lake and chert (silica-rich crystalline sedimentary stone) from around Munsungan Lake north of Mount Katahdin, not to mention the Canadian Maritimes, they also made use of stone from such faraway places as Mount Jasper in New Hampshire, the Champlain Basin of Vermont, western New York, Pennsylvania and even Ramah Bay in northern Labrador. Clearly, these people had far-ranging contacts. Such objects no doubt had special significance, not just on account of their foreign origin, but also because of their distinctive colors and history of how they came into the possession of the person who used them. They served to connect the user with the wider physical and mythological world in which he or she lived.

An idea of what life in a Paleo-Indian camp might have been like. *Collection of the author.*

The Archaeological Background

With few exceptions, Paleo-Indian sites are small and were occupied briefly (but often repeatedly) by small groups of people, perhaps one or two families together. Representative is the Michaud Site, located by the Lewiston-Auburn airport. Here, on sandy soil next to what was once a swamp—a favorite kind of campsite—eight or nine clusters of artifacts were left where people put up their shelters and carried out various activities. Three such spots, for example, are the remains of a shelter on either side of which were outside activity areas. In one of these, points were manufactured and replaced in refurbished bone or wooden hafts. In the other, game was processed and hides were transformed into such things as clothing, bedding and bags.

Periodically, the small groups of Paleo-Indians would come together in larger encampments, as at the famous Bull Brook site near Ipswich, Massachusetts, where they gathered for a communal caribou hunt and to trade, find marriage partners and socialize. Clearly, they were a highly mobile people, but we should not think of them as rootless wanderers. To survive exclusively by foraging for wild foods, people must have detailed knowledge of a region—the kind of knowledge that comes only from lifelong familiarity. Moreover, it is clear that they returned repeatedly to particular favored spots. Their home territories may have been large, but like all historically known hunting and gathering people, they no doubt felt a deep sense of connection with their homelands.

THE ARCHAIC PERIOD

By eight thousand years ago, the climate had warmed to the point that the woodlands of Maine and New Brunswick began to take on something of the characteristics of the mixed deciduous-coniferous forests with which we are familiar today. As a consequence, the arctic and sub-arctic animals that Paleo-Indians hunted had either moved north (like the caribou) or became extinct (like the mammoths). In the new forests, deer, moose and a variety of small animals became abundant, and a wide range of plant foods were available for several months of the year. Various kinds of fish, too, became abundant in bodies of both fresh and salt water. As people adjusted to these new conditions, they developed different practices tailored to interior and coastal living. These changes usher in what archaeologists refer to as the Archaic Period, which dates between roughly nine thousand and three thousand years ago.

The earliest archaeological material of this period that we have from the coast comes from sites that are now submerged beneath forty or more

The "Anderson biface," one of the eight-thousand-year-old bifaces dragged up in Blue Hill Bay by scallopers. This may have been a preform intended to be finished off into a spear or knifepoint. By this time, points were no longer fluted but completed by fine, parallel flaking. *Courtesy John Crock.*

meters of water. One such site is near a now-submerged channel of the Union River in Blue Hill Bay, southwest of Mount Desert Island. Here, in the 1990s, scallopers dragged up stone tools like the 8,000-year-old biface illustrated above. Investigators later discovered a nearby lake (also drowned), formed during a slow period of sea level rise between 11,500 and 8,000 years ago. The landscape would have been an attractive one to people living off fish, game and wild plants.

Another early site, this one not submerged, is at Dresden Falls (which are now submerged) on the Kennebec River. Although the site's existence has been known for a quarter of a century, only recently has its true significance become apparent. Preliminary investigation has revealed that here was a village covering somewhere around twenty acres that was occupied seasonally between about 9,000 and 4,500 years ago. There are only two other similar sites of this period in all of New England. Garbage pits and intact hearths have preserved a variety of plant, fish and animal remains, including sturgeon, striped bass, salmon, muskrat, turtles and moose or deer. Stone projectile points, pieces of whetstones, gouges, adzes, axes, scrapers and slate knives have also been found. Though the site awaits a more thorough investigation, it is now protected by the Archaeological Conservancy, with the help of funds from Land for Maine's Future and the Friends of Merrymeeting Bay.

Limited though our present knowledge is, it appears that people who spent much of the time moving about between small campsites gathered here to catch migrating fish on their annual runs. At the time, sea levels were lower than today, and the first falls of the Kennebec were located between Swan Island and Dresden. As yet, there was no channel on the other side of the island; not until about five thousand years ago were sea levels high enough to drown the falls and create the second channel. It was the perfect place to catch the fish; their abundance, large size and predictability allowed such a large gathering there.

A noteworthy observation is that styles of projectile points at this site are similar to those found at sites west of the Kennebec but are unlike those farther east, suggesting the presence of an ancient ethnic boundary. What makes this intriguing is that this was later the border between Etchemins and Abenakis. The possibility is that this ethnic boundary is quite ancient. To the east of the boundary up into New Brunswick, stone projectile points are not particularly distinctive, nor are they common. It may be that heavier reliance on resources in coastal waters favored use of nets, traps and spears tipped with bone.

Another site of the same vintage as Dresden Falls that has been intensively investigated is on Meddybemps Lake at its outlet, the Dennys River. From here, there was easy access to the Saint Croix River and Passamaquoddy Bay, not to mention the waterways of interior Maine and New Brunswick. People first camped here around 8,600 years ago, living in circular shelters dug into the ground, with a pole framework covered with bark or hide. From their encampment, they exploited the alewife spawning runs; fished for perch, suckers and eels; and hunted or trapped a variety of mammals, birds and turtles. They also gathered various seeds, nuts and other plants. The quantity of food remains, as well as the presence of storage pits, shows that people were not just living day to day but also planning for the seasons ahead. Occupied seasonally between the spring alewife run until fall, this place was visited repeatedly over a period of 400 years or so.

Four artifacts from the now-submerged Lazygut Island site. *On the left*: two bifacially flaked tools of red mudstone, one with a highly polished end. *On the right top*: ground slate ulu, and below it a ground stone adze. Slate knife fragments from Dresden Falls are from tools like this ulu and were probably used to process fish. *Courtesy Steven Cox.*

Moving forward in time, another submerged site off Deer Isle in Penobscot Bay, near the Lazygut Islands, dates to the Middle Archaic Period, around 6,100 years ago. At the time, sea levels were still eight meters below where they are now. Thus, what today is sea bottom was then a broad mudflat behind a granite headland. The location was a good one, with a well-drained spot for a shelter, abundant shellfish nearby and access to the open sea. From this site, scallop draggers, as well as divers from the Maine State Museum, have recovered large, worked oyster shells; a semi-lunar knife, or *ulu* (the term used by the Inuit for similar knives), made of slate; a rhyolite "preform" (stone that has been flaked but had not yet been finished to produce a specific tool); and other implements. Two ground ulus and a full channel gouge have also been pulled up from drowned sites in Passamaquoddy Bay.

The ground slate ulus just mentioned, along with fragments of similar implements from the Dresden Falls site, are representative of technology new in the Archaic Period. Although people continued to make flaked stone tools, ground slate cutting tools were superior for processing the soft flesh of fish as they were split for drying. The smooth edge of the slate knife does not tear the meat the way the nicked edge of a flaked chert knife will. Ground slate also does a better job of scraping the hides of marine mammals, which are more difficult to clean than those of land mammals, owing to the adherence of blubber. A smoother edge permits exertion of pressure over a large area without damaging the hide.

The drawback to ground slate is that it dulls easily and must be frequently resharpened. This is easily done with a whetstone, however, as opposed to the re-flaking required to resharpen a flaked stone knife. In the process, the chipped stone knife is more rapidly "used up" than one of ground slate.

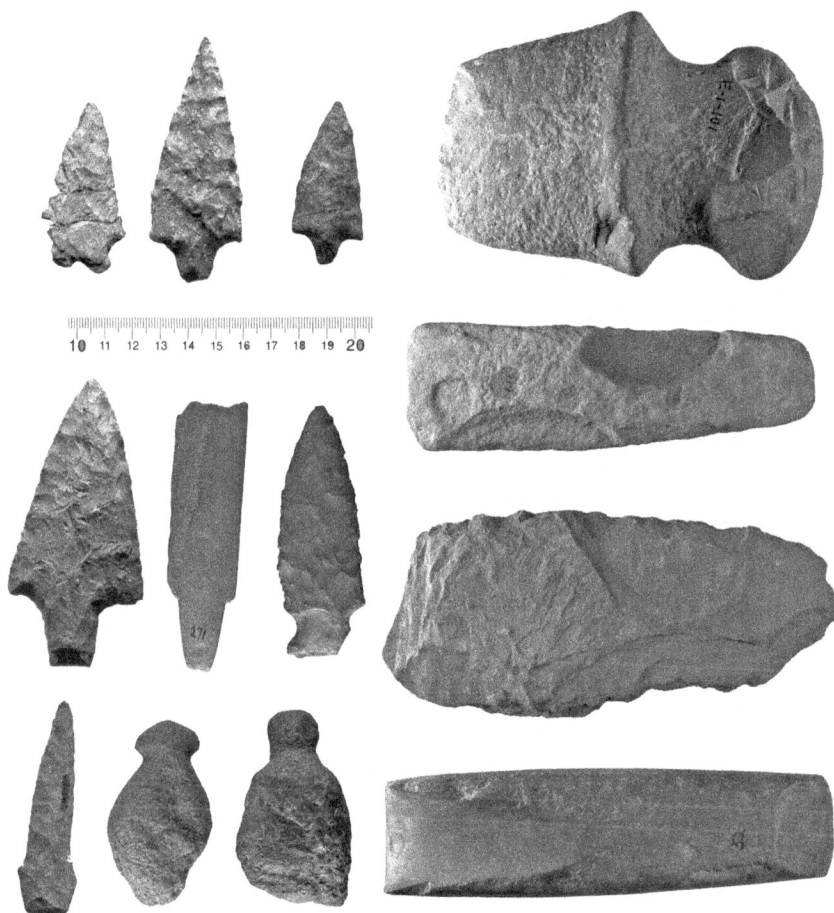

A selection of Archaic stone tools. In the second row middle is a slate point; on the right are a grooved axe, adze and gouges. *Courtesy Arthur Spiess, Maine Historic Preservation Commission.*

Another innovation in the Archaic Period was the production of various implements by "pecking" (with a hammerstone) and grinding (using a sand abrasive) rocks that were often quite hard. In this manner, people made a variety of axes, adzes and gouges out of sturdy volcanic stone for heavy-duty woodworking. These tools are often assumed to have been used to make dugout canoes, but they were probably employed in other tasks, such as sharpening stakes for fishweirs. For sharpening gouge bits, stone rods were used. Ground stone plummets were made to serve as weights on fish lines and nets, as well as for bolas.

By Late Archaic times (6,000–3,500 years ago), exploitation of marine resources had become particularly intense along the coast. In their canoes,

This page: Shown here are the remains of the five-thousand-year-old fish weir located at the outlet of Sebasticook Lake in central Maine and the kind of mallet used to drive stakes into the mud. *Mallet is from the collection of the Deer Isle-Stonington Society; Fish weir photo is courtesy of the late James Petersen.*

using a variety of bone-tipped spears, harpoons, lines with barbed bone hooks, nets and apparently weirs, people were catching all sorts of fish: cod, swordfish, sturgeon, flounder, sculpin, tomcod, herring, salmon, pollock, haddock, striped bass, dogfish and alewives. Most abundant in their garbage are bones from very large cod and swordfish. Their prowess as swordfish hunters was most impressive, for these fish are large and can cause damage to small boats (though they are not as fierce as often made out). Moreover, there were dangers to venturing out on marine waters, where weather conditions can change rapidly for the worse.

Besides finfish, these people also utilized clams (for bait as well as to eat), blue mussels, sea urchins and quahogs. Most shellfish were gathered in late winter and early spring when other food was scarce. It was not a preferred food. Although fish provided the bulk of what people ate in the summer and fall, they supplemented this by hunting seals, ducks and swans. Deer were hunted from late fall to May, and some moose, bear and sea mink (a now extinct, cat-sized animal) were procured as well.

Associated with this coastal adaptation were some of North America's earliest elaborate burial practices. In special cemeteries, the dead were placed in graves, often with copious amounts of red ocher (iron oxide, popularly known as "red paint") and a variety of artifacts, some of which had seen earlier use. These include fire-making kits of rhyolite and pyrite (the prehistoric equivalent of flint and steel "strike-a-lights") wrapped in birch bark or kept in clam shell containers. Other objects seem to have been specially made for interment. These include long, delicate ground slate bayonets that show no wear and are often too fragile to have seen any use. Thought to be imitative of swordfish bills, they may have been widely traded. Their distribution extends beyond that of the cemeteries (between the Kennebec and Saint John

This page: Two techniques used by hunters in the Archaic Period include the use of an atlatl to throw a spear over greater distances with greater force than possible with a handheld spear and the use of bolas to capture birds. *Collection of the author.*

Rivers). In fact, they are more common in Nova Scotia than New Brunswick, but they are only found in the western part of that province. The greatest number is found closest to where the distance to the Maine coast is shortest.

Because the placement of red pigment in graves has often been practiced by peoples in various parts of the world and at various times, archaeologists long ago abandoned the use of the term "Red Paint People" in connection with these cemeteries. The preferred term today is "Moorehead Complex," after Warren K. Moorehead, the archaeologist whose excavations of these graves in the early twentieth century captured the public imagination. Today, we can only speculate on the significance that was attached to the red pigment, but historically in northeastern North America, redness connoted animate, emotive aspects of life. Ocher, too, has practical applications. The iron salts have antiseptic and deodorizing properties, and in native Australia, ocher was used on the living to heal sores, wounds and pains, both internal and external. An individual might also be covered with ocher and placed in the sun to promote sweating.

Moorehead complex graves have also produced our earliest examples of what might be called art in the region. This consists of incised designs on moose-bone daggers from the Blue Hill cemetery and on bayonets from the Cow Point cemetery in New Brunswick.

The earliest elaborate burial in North America is in a 7,500-year-old mound in southern Labrador. Besides red pigment, this and other so-called Maritime Archaic burials from Labrador and Newfoundland share a number of features in common with those from Maine. In some Maritime Archaic graves are Maine bayonets, and several bone artifacts from a cemetery in Blue Hill closely resemble Maritime Archaic artifacts. Moreover, flaked stone tools made of chert from Ramah Bay in Labrador are frequent in Moorehead Complex graves. In fact, the Moorehead Complex and Maritime Archaic overall shared many technological elements: similar tools of bone and ground stone. Different are their flaked stone tools; for the most part, those from Maine and New Brunswick resemble those of southern New England. Their dietary preferences differed, too; Maritime Archaic people emphasized marine mammals more than cod and swordfish.

In addition to the elements shared with the Maritime Archaic, the people here on the coast had a number of things in common with their contemporaries in interior Maine and New Brunswick. In fact, typical Moorehead Complex flaked stone points have been found at sites in northwestern Vermont, and stone from the Champlain Valley in Vermont was sometimes used to make tools here on the coast. Moreover, the occasional copper adze, gouge and spear point, all imports from the Great Lakes, have been found here on the coast. Thus, in spite of their year-round residence near the sea and their focus on local marine resources, Late Archaic people here were fully aware of what was going on in the wider region and maintained regular relations with other people, including some who lived quite far away.

THE END OF THE ARCHAIC PERIOD

By 3,800 years ago, the rate of sea level rise had slowed again, and a hardwood forest more like those of the south than today's coastal forest was well established on the land. In the Gulf of Maine, increased tidal action (a consequence of higher sea level) resulted in cooler water temperature and the disappearance of swordfish and quahogs. Oysters survived only up warmer coastal estuaries, one of the more notable being the Damariscotta River. With these changes, people altered their subsistence practices to take advantage of abundant land resources. On North Haven Island in Penobscot Bay, for example, when swordfish hunting ended, deer hunting became especially prominent. Moose were hunted, too, along with a number of smaller mammals and birds. Important plant foods included butternuts, hickory, walnuts, beechnuts and acorns, the latter being roasted on stone pavements. Still, marine resources were not neglected altogether, as people continued to gather clams; to catch cod (but in the fall, rather than summer), flounder and some other in-shore fish; and to hunt seals. It's just that fish were less prominent in the diet than before.

Associated with these changes in subsistence was a new technology, known as the Susquehanna Tradition. As its name implies, it shares many elements with technologies south of New England, and its spread northward in Maine has been interpreted by some as a consequence of southern people moving into the region. This is unlikely, however, as people continued to occupy the same sites they had all along, doing many of the same things they had always done. Not only are there continuities between Susquehanna and earlier materials, but also Susquehanna tools in Maine are virtually never made from foreign stone, even though stone from Maine sources was frequently used by Susquehanna people living to the south. Nor are all the southern Susquehanna elements present in Maine. As one goes eastward into New Brunswick, Susquehanna elements are relatively rare beyond the Saint Croix River, as one might expect if these were borrowed elements from the south.

In short, it looks as if people here, while adapting to altered environmental conditions at home, adopted a number of innovations made by people living south of them, incorporating them into their own repertoire. Anthropologists have known for a long time that technological elements are easily borrowed from one people by another, whereas the introduction of such core elements of culture as beliefs, values and ways of relating to one another are commonly strongly resisted. Nor was this the first time people here did this; the previous Moorehead Complex, for example, was an outgrowth of earlier indigenous elements enriched by borrowings from people living in southern New England, interior Maine and New Brunswick, as well as around the Gulf of Saint Lawrence. Moreover, as we have seen, from the time of their first arrival in Maine and the Maritimes, people maintained contacts with other people from away.

Further evidence of population continuity, even as their cultures changed, is suggested by the geographical distribution of Moorehead Complex cemeteries. Stretching from the Kennebec to the Saint John River, this closely matches the extent of the historic Etchemin homeland.

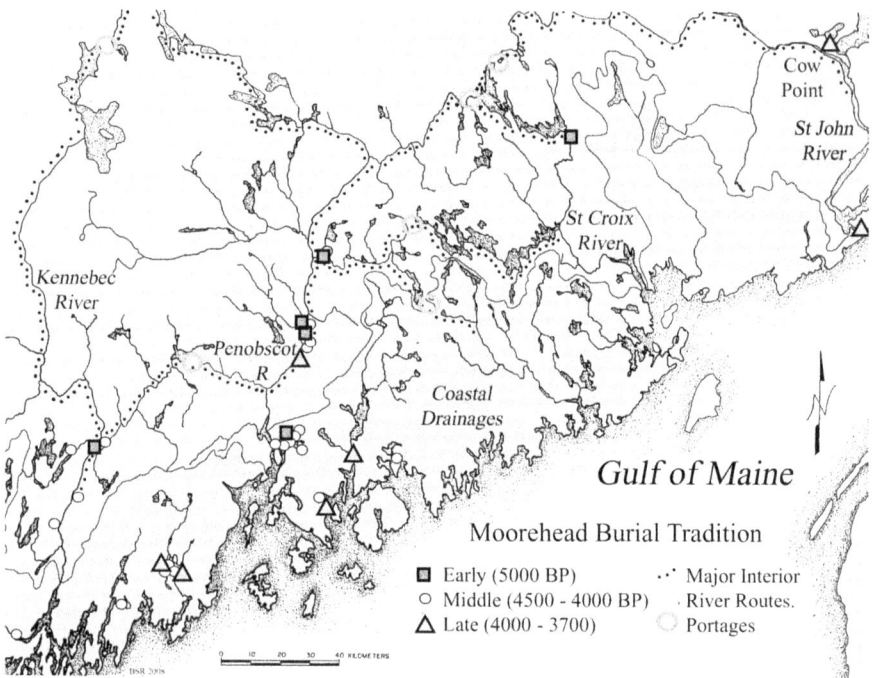

Distribution of Morehead Complex cemeteries. *Courtesy of Brian S. Robinson.*

Several of these cemeteries even show continued use by those responsible for Susquehanna technology.

Susquehanna sites that have been excavated include one on North Haven and others at Naskeag and Eddington. Distinctive are notably broad but thin stone projectile points with stems or side-notched near the base. Unlike their predecessors, Susquehanna tool makers carried out the early stages of stone flaking at quarry sites, such as Mount Kineo, leaving the finishing touches to be made as needed wherever people happened to be at the time. This meant that much of the weight of raw material didn't have to be carried around, as it was left behind in the form of waste flakes from initial reduction. Bone technology changed, too. In earlier times, bone was worked by scraping, but now it was worked by grinding and polishing. Objects of bone included not only utilitarian items such as harpoon and spear points but also decorated combs and pins, as well as hemispheric gaming pieces not unlike a sort of dice used historically by the Penobscots.

Like their predecessors, Susquehanna people continued to bury their dead in special cemeteries, and they placed red ocher in the graves. In several cases, these graves penetrated others of the earlier Moorehead Complex. Although some have interpreted this as a lack of knowledge of the presence of the earlier interments, it may just as well be an example of a practice seen historically. Among the Penobscots, more recent graves in a cemetery would penetrate older ones, on the belief that enlargement of the cemetery to accommodate new graves would cause deaths to fill the new space. Also placed in Susquehanna graves were objects of flaked stone, similar to (but of higher quality than) tools found in other contexts. Points, for example, were generally longer and wider relative to their thinness. Bones of edible animals, as well as nuts, were also placed in graves, as were copper beads. Other practices, new in this era, were cremation, the burning of fires over interments and occasional digging up of whole or partial skeletons to be combined in bundles for reburial or cremation.

THE CERAMIC PERIOD

Sites of this period, which began about three thousand years ago, are numerous along the coast, both on islands and the mainland, with over two thousand known from the state of Maine alone. Most are shell middens, made up of huge numbers of shells, mostly from soft shell clams, mixed with other refuse discarded by the people who camped there. Although some are quite small—the Scott's Midden site on Deer Isle measures a mere three hundred square meters—they range in size up to large ones like the Indiantown Island site in the Sheepscot River Estuary, which covers more than three thousand square meters, or the even larger Damariscotta shell middens. Some nine meters deep (most of the shell middens are no more than two meters deep, if that), the Damariscotta middens are unusual not only for their depth but also for their composition: oyster, rather than clamshells.

The Ceramic Period (called the Woodland Period in the rest of New England and Canada), as the name implies, is marked by the appearance and development of pottery containers. Up until this time, people had used bark, wood and skin containers for carrying, cooking and storage. The big advantage of clay pots was that they could be placed directly in a fire to cook stews and soups. No longer did people have to rely on the technique of heating up rocks to then drop into food held in an otherwise flammable container.

The disadvantage of clay pots, besides being breakable, heavy and bulky to transport, is that they require a great deal of time and effort to make. Although clay was readily available, it had to be gathered and transported to the work area. There, it had to be cleaned by hand and worked to the proper consistency. Then rotten granite was collected and burned so that it could be pulverized into grit of the right consistency to mix into the clay for temper. All of this took hours over several days, and the combination of wet clay and sharp grit in the mixing took its toll on the potter's hands.

Each pot was built up as coils of the clay were placed one above another, welded together and then "paddled" with a wooden tool, sometimes covered with fabric of plant fiber, to drive out air bubbles. Decoration was impressed in the wet clay using various round and dentate ("tooth like") wooden tools and cord-wrapped sticks. The pot was then left to dry. Meanwhile, a great deal of wood had to be gathered for firing, another time-consuming activity. On the coast, driftwood was probably the most available fuel.

Before the final firing, the pots had to be preheated to drive off the "pore water" that remained in the clay even after drying in the air. Without this, the pot would explode when fired. It had to be heated enough to "smoke" (as pore water turned to steam) but not so hot as to shatter or crack. For the final firing, a long pit was dug to control the draft, and wood was heaped over the pots and set afire. This was best done at night when there was less wind and incandescence of the pots was easily observed. When they reach a temperature of six hundred degrees, necessary to transform clay to pottery, the vessels light up.

The Archaeological Background

This latter phenomenon, which signals the change from soft, water-soluble clay into hard ceramic that does not disintegrate in water has led archaeologist Charles Paquin, who has replicated this technique of pottery making, to suggest that the first pottery had a special, perhaps ritual significance. It must have appeared magical as the pot seemed to glow from within as it transformed from one state to another. In keeping with a ritual significance, early pottery vessels, though distributed widely, occur only in limited quantities at any given site and were sometimes included in human burials.

The earliest pottery, known as "Vinette I" is just like that made elsewhere in the Northeast at the time and was clearly adopted by the locals from outside the region. The pots are generally small, with pointed bases so that they could be set snugly into the coals of a fire.

Although the earliest pottery was rarely decorated, the situation changed around 2,150 years ago. For the next 500 years, people elaborately decorated smooth exterior surfaces using stamping tools such as dentate or pseudo-scallop-shell forms. These were rocked back and forth on the still damp clay. This pottery represents a peak not only in terms of decorative elaboration but also in technological proficiency. Never again were pots made in this region with thinner, harder walls.

Between 1,650 and 950 years ago, although vessel shape remained essentially the same as before, there was a wider range of sizes, some holding up to two gallons. Vessel walls were thicker, grit was coarser and the coils less securely joined than before. As for decoration, pseudo–scallop shell was gone, whereas tooth size on dentate stamping tools increased.

By around 1,350 years ago, dentate stamping, too, disappeared

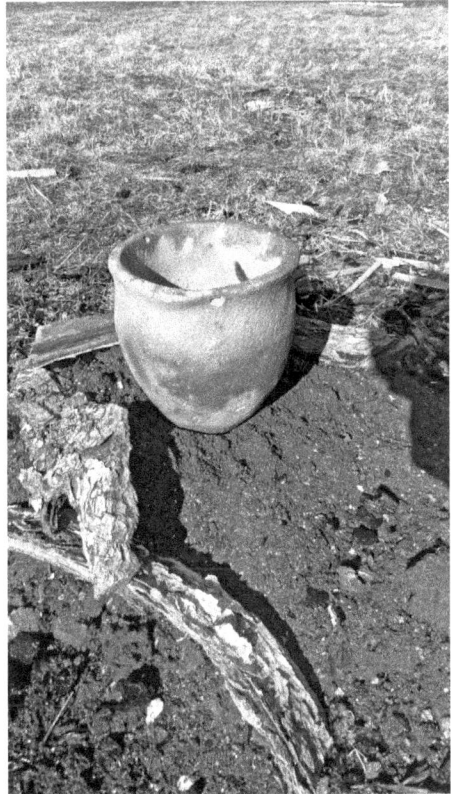

This replica of a Vinette I pot was made by Charles Paquin by the same techniques used by Indians in the Early Ceramic Period. *Collection of the author.*

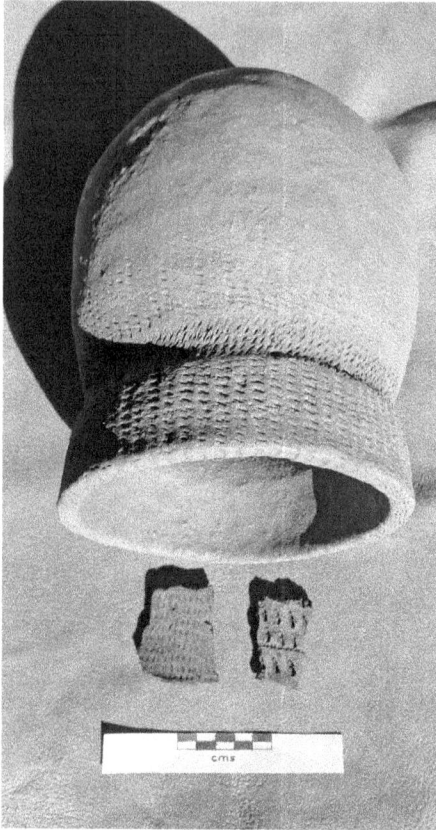

A replica of a pot, made by Charles Paquin, with cord-wrapped stick decoration and sherds from ancient vessels. *Collection of the author.*

in favor of exterior decoration with cord-wrapped sticks combined with systematically placed, discreet punctuation. Generally, this was confined to the vessel's upper part. Twist of the cordage used in decoration reflects an old distinction between coastal and interior people. The cordage was made by twisting plant fibers together, and on the coast, people habitually twisted these to the left (so-called Z-twist). In the interior, they twisted to the right (S-twist). Textiles similarly show a Z slant of the weft on the coast but an S slant in the interior. These habits, once learned, are so deeply ingrained that they seem the "natural" way to do it, even though one is no more natural than the other. But once established, the pattern is passed from one generation to the next and is relatively impervious to change. Historically, such differences are usually associated with ethnic differences.

Further changes in ceramic technology were underway around 950 years ago. On the coast (but not inland), ground shell temper replaced grit. There was, however, a resurgence of the latter around 650 years ago. At the same

The Archaeological Background

This Passamaquoddy crooked knife may be compared with the beaver-tooth knife in the next photo. *Collection of the author.*

time, more globular forms began to replace the old pointed-base type. Vessels also became dramatically thinner again, sometimes with fancy collars of the sort seen on Iroquoian ceramics in New York, Ontario and Quebec. While cord-wrapped-stick decoration continued, incised decoration, often added to the vessel surface by various noncylindrical tools, became more common. Although native ceramics continued to be made until about 250 years ago, those made over the final 150 years show some imitation of European forms.

As ceramic technology underwent change over the past three thousand years, so too did lithic technology. A marked decline in numbers of ground-stone tools may relate to replacement of dugout by bark canoes, although this assumption has recently been called into question. Bark or even skin-covered canoes could be older. Numbers of small scrapers of flaked stone probably were used in constructing bark canoes, as were beaver teeth. The latter, present in large numbers, are precursors of the "crooked knives" used historically by native people in canoe construction and for other wood carving.

Flaked stone tools generally show a great deal of random variety. Between 3,000 and about 2,150 years ago, projectile points included forms similar to side-notched ("Meadowood") and stemmed ("Adena") points made by people in New York and Ohio. Often, these were made from Kineo rhyolite and Munsungan chert. As time wore on, these forms gave way to a variety of generally small side-notched, corner-notched and triangular points. Some of these were deliberately made to break on impact, thereby acting like shrapnel. By increasing the severity of the wound, it enhanced the probability of a successful kill. These points were used on the ends of arrows, reflecting a change in hunting weaponry. Sometime between 1,000 and 2,000 years ago, the bow and arrow replaced the spear and spear thrower as the primary killing weapon.

Although a spear thrown with a spear thrower can kill at distances of up to eighteen to twenty-seven meters, an arrow shot from a bow is effective up to ninety-one meters. Not having to get so close to the game, with less movement to get off a shot, meant that the animal was less likely to sense

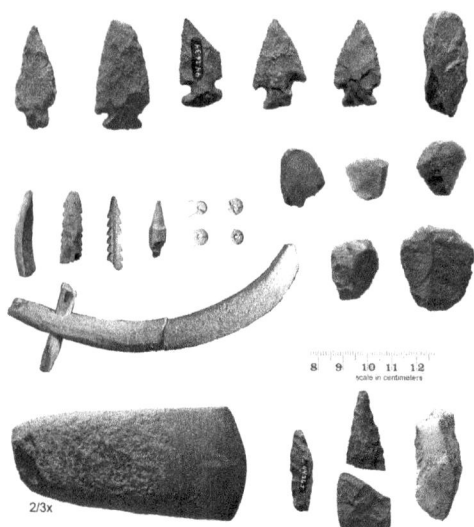

A selection of Ceramic Period stone and bone objects, including a beaver-tooth knife with an antler handle (next to bottom). *Courtesy Arthur Spiess, Maine Historic Preservation Commission.*

danger and flee. What's more, a bow with a quiver of arrows is easy to carry and shoots truer at close range. Truly, this was an innovation that greatly enhanced a hunter's chance of success.

Bone technology flourished in the Ceramic Period. Objects included simple bone points, probably used on the ends of arrows and fish spears (in Deer Isle sites, these are often associated with flounder bones). Beaver teeth, used for woodworking, are common, as are barbed spears and harpoons. Other bone objects consist of hooks, awls, needles, beads and perforated animal teeth.

The people responsible for this technology continued to live, as did their forebears, as foragers of wild foods. Marine protein accounted for much of their diet and included fish, birds and mammals. A study of food remains from the Indiantown Island site reveals that people would come to this place in the winter and subsist on clams, deer, tomcod and seabirds, while waiting for spawning cod to arrive. Then, into the early summer, fishing became dominant. Overall, clams provided roughly 90 percent of the meat in the diet, with cod in second place and mammals (mostly deer) in third place. These staples were supplemented by a wide variety of other mammals, birds and fish.

The Archaeological Background

Table I-1
ANIMAL REMAINS FROM INDIANTOWN ISLAND

Mammals	**Reptiles**	**Birds**	**Fish**
Deer Moose Bear Gray Seal Harbor Seal Porpoise Dog Beaver Porcupine Hare River Otter Fisher Lynx or Bobcat Sea Mink (now extinct) Mink Raccoon	Turtle (2 kinds)	Loon Canada Goose Cormorant Great Auk (now extinct) Murre or Razorbill Auk Eagle Small Duck Medium Duck Large Duck	Cod Haddock Sturgeon Pollock Dogfish Cunner Sculpin Tom Cod Yellowtail Flounder Dab (Flounder) Winter Flounder Goosefish Hake

A similar diet was seen at the Kidder Point site, on the west shore of Penobscot Bay, near the mouth of the river. By contrast, farther out on the bay, at North Haven Island and sites farther Down East on Passamaquoddy Bay, consumption of cod declined over time, while that of flounder, sturgeon and other in-shore species (such as striped bass and sculpin) increased. These were probably taken in nets and weirs. There was also intensification of seal hunting, of both gray and harbor seals, not only in mating and pupping seasons (as in late Archaic times, when they were killed on the ice or in rookeries), but also throughout the summer when they were pursued in open water. In addition, the occasional whale and porpoise were taken. In the case of whales, one or two might be procured in a year, with the meat and blubber being widely shared among several bands. Also hunted were sea mink and a variety of water birds, including (especially after about AD 1000) great auks (penguin-like birds, now extinct).

As seals and fish were the mainstays of the summer diet, deer and moose dominated that of the late fall and winter. Over time, the size of deer taken decreased, and the numbers of moose killed increased dramatically. Reasons for this include stress on the deer population from hunting pressure, as well as a change in coastal forest composition caused by a cooler climate. This change, which took place between 1,500 to 1,000 years ago, saw the spread of spruce forests along the coast creating conditions favorable for moose. Furbearing species, too, were increasingly preyed upon, implying the existence of a sophisticated trapping technology. In the case of beaver, all ages and sexes were taken; apparently, entire lodges were cleaned out. So abundant are beaver remains, especially in sites of the late Ceramic Period, that people must have been getting substantial numbers from the interior, presumably through trade. Some bear were hunted, from late fall through spring. And as before, edible and medicinal plants were collected in season.

Although archaeologists today try to avoid disturbing burials out of respect for native people, some information comes from older excavations as well as instances where graves are accidentally disturbed by construction or natural erosion. We know that rituals surrounding death changed in the Ceramic Period, as elaborate burial ceremonialism gave way to simpler burial practices. Customs in Maine are less well known than those elsewhere in Vermont and the Maritimes, where elaborate treatment of the dead reached its peak between 3,000 and 2,150 years ago. Indeed, during this time period, practices seen earlier there spread to the Midwest, where they were further elaborated in Adena and Hopewell mound burials. Influences from the Midwest, in turn, came back to influence practices here in the Northeast.

In Vermont and the Maritimes, several cemeteries of this Early Ceramic Period are known in which red ocher, numerous beads and other objects of copper (from Nova Scotia), shell beads, tubular smoking pipes of lithified Ohio fireclay (with tobacco residue in them) and numerous objects of both ground and flaked stone were placed in the graves with the deceased. Many of the objects were made of materials that were traded, sometimes in finished forms, from places as far afield as the Gulf of Mexico to the south, Ohio and Indiana to the west, northern Quebec and Nova Scotia. Although the cemeteries represent an in situ development from earlier practices, that development was enriched through contacts with other people.

As was the case with the red pigments placed in Morehead complex cemeteries, we cannot be certain of the significance of the copper and shell objects placed with the deceased. They may have been purely for the sake of ornamentation, but historically in the Northeast, bright reflective substances such as copper and shell were associated with physical and spiritual well-being and were regarded as gifts of underwater grandfathers.

Along the coast, Early Ceramic Period cemeteries like those just discussed appear to be rarer than in what historically was Mi'kmaq country. One is in Maine near Lake Alamoosook in Orland. Unfortunately, it was excavated early in the twentieth century by rather crude methods. Evidently, the Ceramic Period graves had intruded into earlier ones of the Moorehead Complex. In three of these graves, the bodies had been laid out on layers of charcoal, along with tubular smoking pipes of Ohio fireclay, small copper beads and red ocher.

Across the border in New Brunswick, beneath a shell midden in Saint Andrews, a burial nearly two thousand years old included numerous copper beads, two giant shark's teeth, two bifaces (flakes removed from both surfaces of the tool), a bipointed object of stone, a cigar-shaped rod, a strike-a-light and five celts. Traces of matting were evident, and red ocher was present. The simplicity of this and of the cemetery in Maine, compared to contemporary cemeteries elsewhere in the Northeast, combined with their rarity, could be a reflection of people on the coast simplifying burial practices. This was a trend well underway in the Middle Ceramic Period. Alternatively, it could simply be a factor of discovery.

The rarity of these burials on the coast compared with other parts of the Maritimes is of interest, given a similar situation in the early era of contact between natives and Europeans. At that time, "copper kettle burials" became popular in Mi'kmaq country. For two hundred years or more, Mi'kmaqs included complete or fragmentary copper or brass kettles obtained from Europeans, along with other items of native manufacture, in graves. In Etchemin country, by contrast, copper kettle burials are rare. Could this differentiation be a later manifestation of differences first seen in the Early Ceramic Period? We don't know, but it is an intriguing possibility.

After about two thousand years ago, burials were not commonly placed in cemeteries away from habitation sites, nor were objects of "exotic" materials regularly placed with them. Instead, inclusions were either basic ones or nonexistent. There was considerable variation in treatment of the deceased, as individuals might be buried singly or bundled up with others, in either extended or flexed positions.

Not much is known about other ritual practices. Depictions of human and animal figures in rock ledges at Machias, however, discussed in the next chapter, attest to the practice of shamanism. The earliest of these images dates back some three thousand years, and they were continuously added to up into historic times. What they depict are visions seen by shamans who had entered states of trance to contact and manipulate various spirit beings.

When entering a trance, the first images seen as visions emerge as various geometric patterns: lattices, nested curves, triangles, zigzags and the like. These tend to persist even as various animals, monsters and other beings emerge in deeper trance. These images may explain the concentric circles and lines that appear on forty incised pebbles recovered from a shell midden at Holt's Pond in Bocabec, New Brunswick. Like the Machias images, they seem to reflect the practice of trancing. The same is true of an incised stone object found at Meductic. Possibly, these stones were regarded as having special supernatural powers and were carried around in "medicine bags." We cannot be sure of this, but it is consistent with historic practices. Moreover, such a medicine bag is known from an Early Ceramic cemetery in Vermont.

Possible evidence of trancing may be seen as far back as the Late Archaic. This is suggested by the lines and zigzags that decorate the previously mentioned slate bayonets and bone daggers found at the Moorehead Complex cemeteries at Blue Hill and Cow Point.

As the earlier discussion of subsistence indicates, people continued to live on the coast year-round. For shelter, they constructed round to oval wigwams consisting of a pole framework that was covered by bark or animal hides. Their presence at a number of coastal sites in both Maine and New Brunswick is indicated by oval, shell-free floors from two to three meters across. These floors were sometimes dug from ten to sixty centimeters into the ground, with shell refuse banking against the base of the walls. Clean sand was periodically spread over the floors. That coastal and interior populations continued to be ethnically distinct is indicated by their plant fiber industries that we know from impressions on pottery.

About one thousand years ago, distinctions between coastal and interior populations begin to blur. Year-round coastal settlement gave way to a more mobile pattern, as people tended to move inland during the winter, returning to the coast for the spring, summer and fall. Associated with this change in settlement was an exponential increase in exotic materials, such as chert from Ramah Bay in Labrador, Onondaga chert from western New York and Ontario, jasper from Pennsylvania, chalcedony from Nova Scotia and copper, also from Nova Scotia. At the same time, fur trading seems to have been on the rise.

On Passamaquoddy Bay about eight hundred years ago, sites on the New Brunswick side of the Saint Croix River were abandoned altogether in favor of locations farther east at Digdeguash Harbor, where the Bonny River, a major travel route, enters Passamaquoddy Bay. This apparently relates to

The Archaeological Background

An artist's impression of a Ceramic Period campsite at Fernald Point, Mount Desert Island. *Painting by Judith R. Cooper. Courtesy Abbe Museum.*

rising sea levels, which increased bank erosion in the abandoned area. The erosion wiped out any productive clam flats, leading people to move to more productive areas. Another distinction of the Saint Croix region was the near disappearance of deer by the end of the prehistoric period.

One of the largest of the warm-season coastal encampments known anywhere on the coast was located at Naskeag Point, by the western entrance to Blue Hill Bay. The location is spectacular; standing on the point, one has an unobstructed 180-degree view of the waters from the estuary of the Union River to the north, all the way to Isle au Haut to the south. Midway between the Kennebec and Saint Croix Rivers, all who passed on the waters could be seen, unless they passed out to sea beyond Swan's and Marshall's Islands and Isle au Haut. This site is remarkable not only for its size and location but also for the nature of its cultural material and its near absence of shells. Over 20 percent of the artifacts are foreign to the region, including side- and corner-notched points unlike those used around Penobscot Bay or Blue Hill Bay and pottery from as far away as Nova Scotia and New Jersey. A thirteen-meter alignment of post molds suggests the presence of at least one longhouse.

Analysis of the unusually large collection from this site indicates that it was an encampment to which people came in the summer and early fall in order to trade with people from distant places. Its mid-coast location made it a strategic spot for people to meet from as far afield as Nova Scotia in the north and Cape Cod in the south. This raises the issue of a Norse coin alleged to come from the site. Unfortunately, precise documentation of the find does not exist, and the person who claimed to have found it was an avid collector of Norse coins. Hence, we cannot rule out the purported find as a hoax. Alternatively, one might suppose it came here through trade from the Norse settlement on Newfoundland, except that the Norse site was abandoned by the time the coin was minted, between 1066 and AD 1085. Of course, it could have been carried to Labrador by people from Greenland, who came there to collect wood, and from there to Maine as native people pursued their regular trade. One thing seems certain: absence of any other objects of Norse origin at Naskeag rules out an actual visitation by these people.

The blossoming of Naskeag as a major trading center corresponds with a cycle of climatic cooling. The change in living patterns, however, probably has more to do with cultural practices than climate. Throughout much of New England, Indian populations began to raise corn, beans and squash. In northern New England, our earliest evidence of these crops comes from a site in Springfield, Vermont, and dates to about AD 1120. On the coast, Indians living west of the Kennebec took up limited farming, but those living farther Down East did not.

That Indians of the Down East coast did not take up farming relates to three factors: shortness of growing seasons, abundance of wild food resources and availability through trade of corn, beans and squash. The latter two allowed people to live well, without having to put in the longer hours of hard work required by farming. Moreover, by accumulating surplus animal hides and furs, as well as copper from the Mi'kmaq mines in Nova Scotia, they could exchange these with their western neighbors for such corn and other crops as desired.

To sum up, the archaeological record is one of indigenous people adapting to changing environmental conditions, as well as influences from other peoples with whom they regularly interacted. By five thousand years ago, a way of life was established that endured for the next several millennia, although not without further changes. One might liken those changes to variations on a basic theme. Many were essentially "cosmetic," the changes in pottery styles being a good example. A few, such as the changes at the end of the Archaic Period, were more momentous, punctuating intervals of considerable stability. Though they appear to be sudden in the archaeological record, they no doubt took at least a few generations to accomplish. Their apparent suddenness was merely relative to what came before and after. In any event, it all led up to the way of life encountered by the first Europeans when they entered the Gulf of Maine some four hundred years ago.

Chapter 2

Life in Etchemin Country at the Dawn of Recorded History

To understand what life was like in Etchemin country (Ketakamigua) before it was disrupted by the arrival of the Europeans, we must engage in a bit of detective work. For one thing, the Indians were a nonliterate people—for them, oral traditions adequately took care of their needs—and so we have no written accounts from them until well into the nineteenth century. Perhaps the most famous of these was written by Penobscot Joseph Nicolar, *The Life and Traditions of the Redman*, published in 1893.

At the time this was written, the future looked pretty grim for Nicolar's people. In North America, the prevailing conviction was that Indians were destined for extinction, and government policies were designed to promote this through assimilation. Concerned that the old storytellers, so important for the transmission of culture, were dying off, Nicolar felt it imperative that he preserve what he knew. Fearful of the loss of his culture, as new generations were becoming assimilated, he wished to ensure that those who came later might learn and understand.

As for accounts written by Europeans, there is virtually nothing until Champlain came along in 1604. By then, the indigenous populations were already feeling the effects of escalating warfare, as discussed in the introduction, and possibly foreign diseases contracted from Mi'kmaqs, who had been in close contact with Europeans for close to seventy-five years. To be sure, a few Europeans had ventured along the coast of the Gulf of Maine before Champlain: Giovanni Verrazano for the French in 1524, Estevan Gomez for the Portuguese a year later, Jean Alfonse for the French in 1542 and the Englishman John Walker in 1580. Yet they provide little information about the people they encountered, save that Verrazano was "mooned" by Abenakis somewhere around Casco Bay and that John Walker stole three hundred dried moose skins on the coast of Penobscot Bay. In fact, this last bit of information is of interest, for it is one piece of evidence for the coastal trade mentioned in earlier sections of this book. Lacking any indication of trade between Indians and Europeans in the bay before Champlain, these hides were probably destined for the corn-growing Abenakis to the west.

Starting with Champlain, we do have considerable information from French sources, although they deal with people in the throes of change and are not free of ethnocentric biases, as when Champlain asserted his belief that "they have no law among them." English accounts began with James Rosier's chronicle of Captain George Weymouth's visit to Penobscot Bay in 1605. Though useful, the English knew the Indians less well than the French and had their share of biases as well. Crucial in fleshing out these early

Artifacts from the Scott's landing site, a small encampment on Deer Isle occupied repeatedly from about three thousand years ago to about four hundred years ago. Shown here are the most recent objects: shell beads, pieces of decorated bone, pottery sherds and a piece of sheet copper or brass. *Courtesy of Stephen L. Cox.*

accounts, in the late nineteenth and early twentieth centuries, folklorists like Charles Leland, linguists like John Dyneley Prince, anthropologists like Frank Speck and the gifted amateur Fanny Hardy Eckstorm collected oral traditions from Penobscot and Passamaquoddy elders. And as previously noted, Indians like Joseph Nicolar began writing their own accounts. Finally, archaeological sites from the Contact Period provide important information. Consequently, we are able to piece together a reasonable picture of what life was like among the Etchemins.

DAILY LIFE

At the start of the seventeenth century, there were perhaps a dozen autonomous communities in Ketakamigua. Highly mobile, these people would periodically stay at favorite locations, never for more than five or six weeks, before moving on to another place. Often, these were small campsites occupied by one or two married couples, but at other times several families would come together at traditional gathering places. The total Etchemin population was never large, perhaps altogether 5,000 people. A single community would consist of between 300 and 500 people ranging over a region of perhaps 1,600 square miles. For example, Mount Desert Island was at the center of one such territory that stretched from Brooklin to Schoodic, taking in the offshore islands as well as the interior watersheds of the rivers

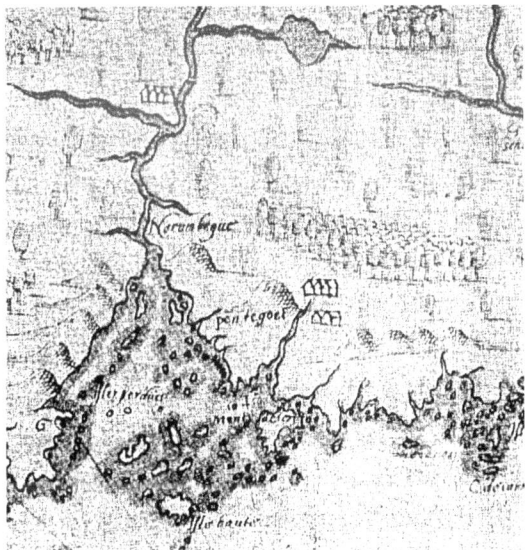

Detail of Champlain's map of New France, 1607, showing Penobscot, Blue Hill and Frenchman Bays. *Courtesy Library of Congress Map Collections: http://hdl.loc.gov/loc.gmd/g3321p. np000002.*

flowing into Blue Hill and Frenchman Bay. A village shown on Champlain's map of 1607 at the falls of the Union River probably was the main village of Asticou, sagamo (chief) of this regional band when the French arrived. Here, people would gather in times of abundance, as they would in the summer at other places such as Manchester Point on Mount Desert Island. An English source reports fifty houses and 150 men at Asticou's village. These "houses" were constructed of birch bark over a pole framework.

Although houses were sometimes larger (as at Asticou's village), the usual Etchemin dwelling was the conical wigwam. To construct them, five or so main poles were set and tied at the top with spruce root. Similar poles were added and reinforced at about head height with a hoop of moosewood. This was held in place with spruce roots and supported a horizontal pole on which various household belongings could be hung. Long sheets of birch bark sewn end-to-end were laid over the pole frame, upper courses overlapping those below. At the top, an opening was left for smoke to escape; in inclement weather, this could be covered by a bark flap. More poles were laid against the outside to hold the bark in place. Inside, the ends of fir boughs were laid on the floor for a soft surface, with piles of skins and mats serving as beds. A tanned moose or deer hide was hung to provide a door.

The first thing that was done when setting up camp was to build a fire. For this, smoldering punk from a rotten hardwood tree was carried around in clay-lined clamshells. This punk burns so slowly that it lasts for about half a day, with hardly any smoke. To kindle a fire, this was placed in dry tinder and blown on. Should the smoldering punk have gone out, a fire could be started from scratch with a fire drill, a spindle with a flywheel of yellow birch, operated by pulling the ends of sealskin strips wrapped around the spindle.

With the fire made, the women would procure and set up the poles for the frame and finish the job of erecting the wigwam. The bark had previously been obtained by the men, in winter when it is thickest. This was rolled up and carried about when moving from place to place. The poles, however were left where they were used. The whole procedure of erecting a wigwam was easily done in a day.

With the exception of winter, when snowshoes were essential, the chief mode of transportation was the canoe, the ideal vehicle for navigating the network of interior lakes, streams and rivers, yet seaworthy enough to venture out on open marine waters. David Cook, author of the definitive book on Indian canoe routes of Maine, described a crossing he made from Grand Manan Island to Nova Scotia with a companion in 1998. On the way, they successfully coped with fog, four- to five-foot waves caused by an incoming tide and a curious minke whale that came close enough to touch with a paddle. All in all, the fifty-mile crossing took ten hours. Although Cook made his crossing in the daytime, it was best done at night, when seas were usually calmer and stars could be used for navigation.

That the Indians were "at home" on the open waters is illustrated by an anecdote about a nineteenth-century steamboat captain who was far out of sight of land when he saw an Indian in his canoe, vigorously waving his arms. Thinking the Indian was lost, the captain maneuvered his vessel up to the Indian only to learn that the man just wanted a match to light his pipe. He knew exactly where he was.

For the Indians, the canoe was the equivalent of today's pickup truck. Ranging in size from eleven to fourteen feet for use in the woods, twelve to eighteen feet for river travel or eighteen to twenty or even twenty-five feet for the salt water, a large canoe weighed about 85 pounds; smaller canoes were lighter. Thus, they were easy to carry when portaging from one body of water to another. As for carrying capacity, a river canoe in which Henry David Thoreau and his Penobscot guide crossed Moosehead Lake in the nineteenth century carried 166 pounds of cargo; with the weight of the two men, the total was around 600 pounds. Larger canoes could carry as many as ten or twelve men. Because they were sewn, canoes had flexibility that modern ones lack, an advantage in rough water. Moreover they were

This nineteenth-century postcard shows Penobscot N.M. Francis and his wife in their canoe. *Courtesy Abbe Museum.*

easily repaired while in use. For this, a container of spruce gum mixed with tallow was carried along. Otherwise, canoeing equipment consisted of paddles of ashwood, a "setting pole" (for poling) and a cup for bailing.

To build a canoe, the first step was to locate a large birch tree that was girdled as high as a man could reach, as well as low near the ground. A vertical slit was then made, and the bark peeled. It was best done in winter, when the bark is heaviest and easily peeled, after the second freeze, using a chisel of fire-hardened wood. As soon as possible after procurement, while still pliable, the bark was bent to shape between two rows of stakes, inner-face down, with stones holding it on the ground along the center. If the bark became stiff, it had to be soaked in warm water to make it pliable again. While working, a nearby fire provided warmth to keep it pliable.

The next step was to sew in place two rails of beechwood for gunwales, using split spruce root for the sewing. Smaller pieces of beechwood were then placed crosswise as thwarts, their ends held by holes in the gunwales, the longest in the center and two or three others placed at intervals in front and behind. These were progressively shorter toward the bow and stern. At these ends, the bark was split and sewn to provide the bend and backed with another piece of bark. Long thin slats of cedar, about four inches wide but tapered at the ends, were then laid in lengthwise to strengthen the canoe. Holding these in place were cedar ribs, bent to shape over a fire and held in place by being fitted into notches in the gunwales. On the outside, the canoe was often ornamented with paint or incision through the dark outside to expose the lighter color beneath.

Besides providing transportation, canoes also could provide shelter. There are numerous accounts of travelers sleeping beneath their overturned canoes overnight or crouching under the overturned canoe to get out of a sudden storm.

The importance of birch bark for the Etchemins cannot be overstated. It not only gave them their canoes and houses but also myriad utensils. This indispensable material was fashioned into a great variety of boxes, baskets, bailers, cups, dips, buckets, kettles, plates, moose calls, torches, hats and even rain ponchos. Not only did the containers hold water, but they could also be used to cook soups and stews. This was done either by dropping hot rocks into the soup or stew, which would bring it to a boil in a surprisingly short time, or by suspending the container over a low fire.

Life in Etchemin Country at the Dawn of Recorded History

Table II-1

USES OF BIRCH BARK

animal calls	games	pipes
armor	grinding sheets	porcupine quill work
bandages	hangings	porringers
baskets	hats	pouches
bedding	house coverings	powder flasks
beds	illustrations	quivers
berry baskets	insulation	raincoats
berry boxes	kettles	rattles
biers	kindling	receptacles
bowls	ladders	sails
boxes	legends	sap containers
buckets	letters	seed testers
cache linings	litters	sewing
canoes	magic	shields
canopies	maple sugar cones	signs
casts for broken bones	maple sugar sap kettles	smoke-hole flaps
clothing	maple sugar spiles	smoke-rack covers
containers	maps	splints
cooking utensils	mats	spoons
cradles	meat bags	stencils
cups	medicine	stone boiling
designs	messages	storage containers
dippers	moose calls	stuffing
dolls	music makers	tinder
doors	muskrat calls	tools
drums	noise makers	torches
dyes	pack baskets	trays
embroidery fans	pails	utensils
figures (totems, etc.)	paint	waterproofing
firewood	paint holders	wigwams
flares	paper	winding sheets
food for dead	patterns	worming
funnels	pillows	wrappers

Butler and Haddock, 1957, courtesy Abbe Museum.

To make these objects, the bark was obtained in the summer, unlike that for canoes and wigwams. It was cut and folded with the dark inner side out and then sewn with spruce roots. A wooden hoop served to stiffen the opening. Containers were often decorated with dyed porcupine quills or, as with the canoes, by scraping or etching designs in the dark outside to expose the lighter color beneath.

Like other historically known people who relied on wild food resources for their subsistence, the Etchemins of the Down East coast enjoyed a highly nutritious diet, were relatively disease-free and had more in the way of leisure time than farmers generally do. The following annual cycle seems to have been typical of the Etchemin way of life. During the spring, with the "spring fish" or "spear fish" moon, families gathered for fishing. Migratory species ranging from alewives to shad and salmon were taken in nets and speared in quantity along the rapids and falls of the various rivers, as at Asticou's village. The spears were tipped with bone, with wooden prongs on either side. These grasped the fish, preventing it from slipping off the point. Sturgeon was caught in the mouths of rivers by harpooning at night. The Frenchman Nicolas Denys described the technique:

Two Indians place themselves in a canoe; the one in front is upright, with a harpoon in his hand, the other is behind to steer, and he holds a torch of birchbark, and allows the canoe to float with the current of the tide. When the Sturgeon perceives the fire, he comes and circles all around, turning from one side to the other. So soon as the harpooner sees his belly, he spears it below the scales. The fish, feeling himself struck, swims with great fury. The line is attached to the bow of the canoe, which he drags along with the speed of an arrow. It is necessary that the one in the stern shall steer exactly as the Sturgeon goes, or otherwise it will overturn the canoe, as sometimes happens. It can swim well, but with all its strength it does not go with fury more than a hundred and fifty or two hundred paces. That being over, the line is drawn in, and it is brought dead against the side of the canoe. Then they pass a cord with a slip-knot over the tail, and they draw it thus to land, not being able to take it into the canoe because it is too heavy.

Although some fish were eaten fresh, many were split and dried or smoked for later consumption. Along the major flyways, waterfowl and the abundant passenger pigeons could be taken in a number of ways by individuals or by groups with nets. Maple trees were also tapped in sugar camps near the village, and the gathering of edible plants intensified as the season progressed.

The June moon, *Muskhogl'gizus* in Penobscot, meaning "seals rise on the water," was a time of large gatherings on the coast for the hunting of sea mammals, seals being of particular importance. Their skins were prized for making bags, and they, along with porpoises and the occasional whale, provided the supplies of fat and grease needed throughout the year. Sea mammals were taken with harpoons similar to those used for sturgeon. Equipped with either toggling or barbed bone points on the end of an eight- to ten-inch foreshaft, this was attached to a longer shaft. James Rosier described how these were used to hunt whales:

> *They go…with a multitude of their boats, and strike him with a bone made in fashion of a harpooning iron fastened to a rope, which they make great and strong with the barke of trees, which they veare out after him: then all their boats come about him, and as he riseth aboue water, with their arrows they shoot him to death; when they haue killed him & dragged him to shore, they call all their chiefe lords together, & Sing a song of ioy: and those chiefe lords, whom they call Sagamos, diuide the spoile, and giue to euery man a share, which pieces so distributed they hang vp about their houses for prouision.*

This diorama at the Abbe Museum at Sieur de Monts Spring in Acadia National Park reconstructs what an Etchemin summer camp would have looked like. *Courtesy Abbe Museum.*

Porpoises were probably taken in a like manner and were cooked by throwing them on an open fire. One contemporary Penobscot recalls his grandmother speaking of children gathering when a porpoise was brought ashore in anticipation of fried porpoise skin, considered a great treat. Seal skin, too, was cut up into small, "chip-like" squares and fried—another great favorite of children. There must have been comparable treats in earlier times.

Spear fishing for flounder, jigging for mackerel and weir fishing were also important activities. One type of weir was a circular arrangement of brush and poles driven into the mud. On a coming tide, a gate would swing open; on the ebb, it would swing closed. Another type was a fence of brush and poles across a stream or other fish passage, with a restricted opening for the fish to pass. Here, they could be speared or netted. Sometimes, these fences were built of stone. One between two islands at Deer Isle in Penobscot Bay resembles another in western Abenaki country, on the Ashuelot River in New Hampshire.

Along with hunting and fishing, the gathering of wild plants continued through summer and early autumn, including such foods as water lilies, milkweed pods, various flowers, roots and tubers from Queen Anne's lace and Jerusalem artichoke, leaves from lambs quarters and burdock and a variety of berries and nuts, such as hazelnuts and beechnuts, to name just a few. The gathering and processing of such items was primarily the work of women.

Plants were gathered not for food alone, however. Oak, hazelnut and Staghorn sumac, among others, were sources of dyestuffs. For fibers and

This postcard from 1935 shows a fish trap across a passage between two islands at Deer Isle in Penobscot Bay. Built of stone, a restricted opening was left where fish would pass, to be speared or netted. *Courtesy Deer Isle–Stonington Historical Society.*

textiles, the inner bark of cedar and basswood, rushes, nettle, Indian hemp, sweet grass, spruce root and wood fibers all were utilized. Basswood was especially good for fish and harpoon lines and nets, being stronger than any other natural fiber rope. It was boiled in water with wood ashes to soften the fibers and extract the slimy juice. Otherwise, the fibers would be stiff and brittle when dry.

Plants were also gathered for medicinal purposes, as the Indians were skilled practitioners of herbal medicine. More than two hundred plants used by Native Americans were at one time or another included in the Pharmacopeia of the United States or the National Formulary, and European settlers in New England frequently sought out native women to cure their ailments.

Another use of plants was to gather eels in late August, when stream flow was low. From pokeberry and Indian turnip root, a poison was made. It took about two days to make enough, at which point a number of people stripped down and went into the water, distributing the poison as they waded, dove and swam. Once their skin started to smart from all the poison, they emerged, treating their sores with plantain leaves. Before long, eels would float belly up, to be gathered by the children and processed by the women. Sun-dried and smoked, the year's supply was gotten in this way.

In many cases, plants, such as cattails, had multiple uses. Young shoots of the plant were eaten in the spring, dried to be made into flour or eaten in the winter and boiled to make a syrup. The pollen was used for flour, the small flowers and seeds were eaten, the leaves were used to weave mats, the stems were used to make darts and knives and the down was used to wrap around infants for warmth. In all, it was a most useful plant!

Land hunting, usually the work of men, was limited and generalized throughout the summer. Deer seem to have been killed only occasionally, though birds and other small game were taken often. From an early English source comes a description of cormorant hunting. On a moonlit night, the Indians paddle out to the rocks where the birds roost. The hunter sneaks up on the "watchman" bird, who stays awake to warn the other birds of danger, and quickly kills it. Then, walking softly among the other birds, he picks them off one by one, wringing their necks. When in molt, ducks are replacing all of their feathers, including those on their wings, and thus are unable to fly. It was during molting season that ducks were driven into coves and up on land, where, unable to fly, they were easily dispatched. Geese were hunted at night, by two or three men in a canoe. They would drift silently into a flock of sleeping birds, whereupon they would light birch-bark torches and make a great deal of noise. The birds were startled into flight, but in their confusion circled around the light, where they were easily clubbed.

The August moon, called *Wikge'gizus* by the Penobscot (meaning "fattening moon"), was a time when seals had put on so much fat that they would remain floating after being killed. August was also the time that medicinal plants were collected and dried because they had reached the height of their power. Again, it was usually the women who were the practitioners of herbal medicine. In September, various types of nuts were collected, ground and consumed immediately. Some, however, were stored for later consumption.

With the coming of the moon, *Madjewado'kigizus* in Penobscot ("animal rutting moon"), the major hunting season began. Most hunting was by small family units that went into the hinterlands to pursue a diversity of animals for both their meat and pelts. Moose and deer were especially important, but smaller game such as porcupine, beaver and hare were taken as well.

A technique probably used by the Etchemin, as it was more recently by the Penobscot, took advantage of the moose in rut. Before dawn, a hunter would position himself in his canoe amidst the reeds at the edge of a pond. There, using a birch-bark cone, he would give some preliminary calls in imitation of a moose cow in heat. After a while, he would increase the intensity of the calls, until he heard a bull moose coming near. At that point, he would dip his bark moose call into the water, then letting the water run out—sounding like the cow's urination in anticipation of the act of mating. With this, the bull hove in sight, to be shot with an arrow by the hunter.

Deer were either stalked, ambushed or taken in snares; smaller game was often taken in traps, including snares and dead falls. Spears and lances were used to kill big game, as was the bow and arrow. The bow was a piece of witch hazel, beech or rock maple about fifty-seven inches long, strung with

This detail from a 1627 engraving depicts a moose hunt on Mount Desert Island. *Prins and McBride 2007:113, courtesy Harald E.L. Prins and Bunny McBride.*

an animal sinew. The arrows were of ash, about two feet long, fletched with three crow or hawk feathers. To carry game and provisions, the hunter had with him a bag of basswood or sealskin. Animal hides were processed as soon after killing as possible. This was the work of women, who stretched the hide for tanning with a mixture of animal brains, bird livers and fish oil.

This focus on hunting and trapping, the drying of meat and the processing of skins for clothing and bedding continued into early winter. As the snow began to accumulate, these hunting parties returned to their winter quarters secure in the knowledge that they had laid in a supply

This statue of an Etchemin woman stands in Saint Croix Island National Park. She is depicted with a cradle board for her infant on her back. *Courtesy John M. Roberts.*

of nuts and other dried foods for the winter. The January moon, called *Pebu'nigizus* by the Penobscots, meaning "winter moon," was the time of the mid-winter feast. It was also a time for repairing gear. Generally, men specialized in woodworking, making bows, arrow shafts (though it was women who fletched them), cradle boards and snowshoe frames. Special care was lavished on cradle boards, which were often exquisitely carved. About two feet long and a foot and a half wide, there was a board at the bottom to hold the infant from slipping off and a hoop at the top. Snowshoe frames were bent ash, four feet long and eighteen inches wide, with two crosspieces. For woodworking, the men had cutting edges of shell, bone and shovel-shaped moose teeth, as well as beaver and porcupine teeth. These were hafted in wood, bone or antler handles, lashed with natural-fiber cordage and secured with resins and animal glues. Wooden mauls, mallets and wedges, drills of bone and stone, bone awls, stone chisels, axes, gouges and hammer stones completed the woodworker's toolkit.

Although men made the frames, it was women who put the webbing in snowshoes. This was done with rawhide, using a bone or wooden needle for the weaving. Different meshes were used for different purposes; an open mesh was best for running down game, but a closer mesh was used for walking. Besides the tasks already noted, women's work consisted of butchering and cooking, the production of clothing and ornamentation and the fabrication of containers of all kinds. They were experts at the use of plant and animal fibers to create bags, mats, cordage and textiles. They were also the ones who transformed leather into pouches and knife sheaths. For her personal toolkit, a woman had awls, needles and scrapers of bone, wood and stone.

As the weeks went by and the dried meat from the fall hunt and other stored food were exhausted, parties went out again to hunt game, particularly deer, which had begun to yard, and moose, which could be run down easily by a hunter on snowshoes, assisted by his dogs. This could be a bleak time of year, however, and if the deer or moose could not be intercepted, or if ice fishing was not good, communities faced periodic threats of famine, particularly during the months of February and March. On the coast, people often resorted to clams to tide them over.

With the coming of spring, the ice broke up in the rivers, lakes and coastal estuaries, and the cycle began again. At this time, a hunter who had been off in the woods would often return home in an expedient canoe made from three or four heavily greased moose hides stretched over a framework of lashed saplings.

For clothing, women made garments of deer, moose or seal hides that were cut and sewn into robes, mantels, loincloths, sleeves and leggings. The thread used for sewing was the sinew that runs along both sides of the spine of deer or moose. Garments were decorated with painted geometric and lace-like designs or embroidered using moose hair and flattened porcupine quills. Quills were also woven into strips for belts and collars. Other decoration consisted of shell-disk beads and little, round copper pieces.

In warm weather, an adult would wear a loincloth, alone if it was really hot or else with a mantle, sleeves and leggings. Sleeves were not attached to other items of clothing but were separate and were tied to each other in front and in back of the body. In cold weather, a thick, fur robe of beaver, otter, raccoon or even bear was added. In all seasons, one's body was liberally rubbed with seal oil or other animal fat to better withstand heat or cold—as well as to ward off black flies and mosquitoes. Footgear consisted of moccasins of moose hide, often reused from old and greasy leather coats, or sealskin. These were decorated with dye and an edging of red and white quills. A high moccasin for winter use was made from the whole skin of a moose foreleg, which has a bend at the knee. This served as the moccasin's heel; the only sewn seam was across the toe.

Adult men wore their hair tied in a knot on the crown of their head. The end of the leather lace used for this hung loose in back. Unlike the Abenakis, they did not shave off their hair far up on the head. Women wore their hair long and loose, unless they were unmarried, in which case it was full-length but tied behind.

Women ornamented their hair with pieces of quill woven into fine leather from moose fetuses strung on a wooden frame and also purple and white shell beads. Men had headdresses of colorful arrangements of bird feathers, beads, dried porcupine quills and moose hair; chiefs would wear a dead kingbird's body spread out on their topknot. Both sexes pierced their ears for pendants of carved bone, shell and stone. Other ornaments were animal teeth and claws. Both sexes also decorated their bodies with red and black tattoos that were thought to confer special spirit power. Faces were painted in red, black and blue colors. Pigments for paints came from red and yellow ocher, charcoal, lignite, manganese and ground white shell. These were fixed with fish roe or egg yolk.

SOCIAL AND POLITICAL ORGANIZATION

The core social unit in Etchemin life was the family band, each of which was associated with a particular animal emblem. Though often referred to today as clans, they should not be confused with the well-known clans of the Iroquois. Etchemin family bands were not based on strict descent through women, as were the Iroquois clans, but rather were more flexible. In Etchemin society, maternal and paternal relatives were of equal importance, and upon marriage, a couple would affiliate with either the husband's or the wife's family, depending on where their prospects looked best and who they got along with better. Thus, family bands were large extended families, consisting of several married couples with relatives in common. At any time, if an individual had a falling out with members of his or her family or saw themselves as having better prospects elsewhere, the couple could transfer to another band in which the husband or wife had relatives.

Each family band was associated with a particular hunting territory, although they did not own this in the sense that people think of ownership today. Family members belonged there, in the same way that the various plants and animals did; it was almost as if the families themselves were owned by their territories. All members of the family had free access to the

Painting by William R. Herries, 1850s, of a Maliseet (Etchemin) Indian camp. In a camp like this, each bark wigwam would be occupied by a married couple with their children. *Library and Archives Canada, Acc. No. 1993-454-59R Lawrence M. Lande Collection.*

territory, but non-members had to ask permission (though there is no reason to suppose that such permission was ever denied).

Family bands were the basic sovereign, organizational units in Etchemin society. The larger community, or regional band, was in effect an association of all those family bands occupying the particular region, like that of Asticou's people. Although individuals were required to marry outside their family bands, frequently it was to someone of the same community. Thus, everyone within a regional band was related to all the others, although neither exclusively through men nor through women.

Because members of a community were all related to one another and interacted on a face-to-face basis, they felt a strong sense of mutual obligation, and there was little need for a formal governing apparatus. Nevertheless, leaders (*sagomos*) did exist, even though they had no power to make decisions and see that people abided by them. Instead, their job was to act as spokespersons for their communities when dealing with outsiders. Internally, leaders could use their powers of persuasion and acknowledged prestige to sway public opinion, and some especially skilled leaders were able to influence affairs in more than their own community. One means to this end was through marriage, extending the range of kinship obligations, and sagamos might have multiple wives. Such individuals, too, were thought to possess supernatural powers. Still, there was no way that they could force people to do what they didn't want to do. Sagamos gained their positions by virtue of their age, wisdom and persuasiveness, as well as by their reputations as good providers. (Asticou's name, for example meant "kettle," perhaps from the feasts he may have hosted.) They also tended to come from particular families with existing reputations for leadership. Leaders remained such only so long as they had people's respect and confidence. Nor were there any real perquisites to office; above all, Etchemin society was strongly egalitarian, sagamos being simply the first among equals. No adult—be it a man or a woman—could tell another what he or she had to do or how to behave.

Although many marriages took place between members of the same regional band, many did not. They not infrequently took place between members of neighboring communities, thus relating people to members of other regional bands. For example, the Baron de Saint-Castin's wife, Molly Matilda, was the daughter of the Etchemin chief Madockawando and a Kennebec woman. (Madockawando's name means "wonder worker" and reflects the belief that he possessed great supernatural power.) Marriages between communities gave people rights of entry to other regional bands, which facilitated trade and made possible cooperation between groups when required for such purposes as defense against a common threat. It also ensured that individuals had people in other regions to whom they could turn for assistance in times of need and that they had a place to live if they found it impossible to get along with members of their own community. In short, boundaries between regional bands were far from rigid, being in fact quite fluid.

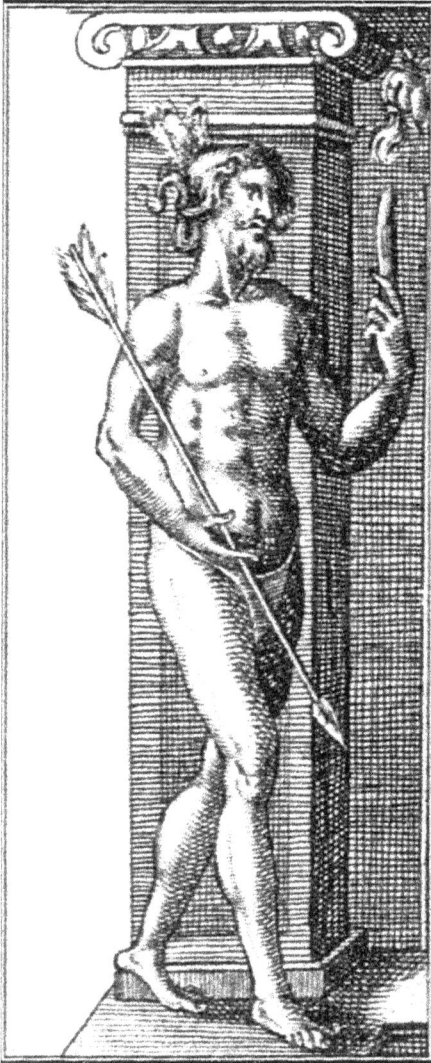

In addition to being strongly egalitarian, Etchemin society was peaceful in nature. This is not to say that violence never occurred, for it may in any human society. Indeed, human skeletons have been found at some archaeological sites—Naskeag, for one—with projectile points embedded in them. But although these people could (and did) fight fiercely if threatened by outsiders, they did not themselves engage in predatory warfare, as did, for example, the Iroquois. Nor were Etchemin villages palisaded, as were those of the Iroquois. As is usual in relatively peaceful societies, individuals grew up with a minimum of conflict; children were not subject to harsh discipline. Here is how Joe Bruchac, an Abenaki, explains it:

Instead of spanking a child when it did wrong, a parent or grandparent would tell one of the old stories which contained the lesson. Physical punishment might be remembered, usually with resentment, long after the misdeed the child did had been

This portrayal of an Etchemin warrior appeared on the title page of Champlain's *Les Voyages* in 1619.

forgotten. But a good story can stay with one for the rest of their life and continue to teach them—at least that is what Indian people believe.

Because storytelling was a favorite pastime, children were constantly exposed to tales that not only entertained but also reminded people of important values. And because children were not excluded from adult activities, they had the examples of their elders around them at all times. Consequently, rarely did adults fail to behave as mature people were expected to behave. In those cases where they didn't, informal pressures were usually sufficient to bring them into line, but when all else failed, persons could be ostracized, requiring them to find some other community willing to take them in.

ETCHEMIN WORLD VIEW

Crucial to the operation of the Etchemin way of life was a belief system in which they saw themselves as parts of, rather than superior to, the natural order. Thus, no great gulf was thought to separate humans from animals and plants; all were seen to be animated by their own inner spirits, and all had to be shown proper respect. This outlook has persisted into modern times, as illustrated by an anecdote told by anthropologist Carlton Coon. In 1928, Coon returned from North Africa with a Riffian from Morocco. During the winter, the two of them traveled to the Penobscot Indian Reservation in Maine, where they stayed with the chief, Gabriel Paul. The Riffian and the chief, both of whom spoke French, had

a wonderful time comparing cultural notes until long into the night... When they were discussing ways to skin animals, Limnibhy [the Riffian] said: "when we kill a sheep, goat, or even a cow, we cut a hole in the skin of a hind leg and blow into it with our mouths while hitting the outside of the body with the flat of a knife that loosens the skin so that you can pull it off over the neck without having to split the skin." To this Gabe replied: "you may do this with tame animals, but you can't with wild ones, because blowing them up makes them look foolish. One of our men once blew up a rabbit that way, and he has never killed another rabbit since."

Among the Etchemin, people who abused the rights of plants and animals by wasting them or failing to accord them proper respect could expect plant and animal spirits to retaliate by sending illness or simply no longer allowing themselves to be killed for human benefit. Similarly, failure to consider the wishes of a variety of other spirit beings was guaranteed to bring trouble down on people's heads. Besides fostering a conservation ethic, these beliefs served as an effective check on deviant behavior.

The way Etchemins related to their environment was clearly reflected in their language. Today, modern versions of that language are still spoken by many Passamaquoddies and Maliseets, whose characteristic ways of structuring words and narratives suggest a participatory relationship with the speakers' surroundings. The following explanation is from a Passamaquoddy-Maliseet dictionary released in 2008:

> *Speakers conceptualized physical space, at whatever scale, in reference to their personal point of view at the moment, that is, in relative terms, not using indicators such as fixed landmarks or latitude and longitude, whose values are independent of human presence. A spatial referent, for example, may be expressed as extending toward or away from the speaker (ckuwawtihiw "on the road toward here," elomaskutek "away over the field") or indicate whether or not an object or event can be seen by the speaker (sakhahte "it extends into view", akuwahte "it is situated out of sight"). Space is active; the perception of the directionality of movement, extension, and orientation gives the surrounding space its structure. In English, for example, a field is usually thought of as a delimited area of open land located in a particular place: a thing, a noun. In Passamaquoddy-Maliseet the notion of field is conveyed by a verb root (-askute-). The verb indicates how land "fields," how an open area lies and extends; field is experienced as a dynamic phenomenon rather than as a static object. Literal translations of weckuwakutek "where it fields toward here" and elomaskutek "where it fields away" suggest the distinctiveness of this way of perceiving. Because all aspects of the physical environment are so constructed, it is unnatural to speak of one's surroundings as separate from the human being experiencing them; people are integral to the world in which they live.*

The physical world of the Etchemins, or "ordinary" or "real human beings," had no beginning. It always existed under the supervision of the Creator of all living things. This Creator made a man and woman out of a piece of stone, but their hearts were hard, and so he broke them up. (Their remains may still be seen in the fields and pastures of the region today.) Taking a piece of living ash, the Creator made another couple, the ancestors of the Etchemins. Like the trees from which the wood came, they are rooted in the earth and, like trees blowing in the wind, could dance gracefully.

After the Creation, the world was made fit for human habitation by a powerful transformer named *Gluskabe*. Raised as an orphan by his grandmother woodchuck, he had many adventures in the course of which he, often through trickery, moderated the force of winter, tamed the more severe rapids, reduced the size of giant animals (a faint memory of ice-age animals like the mammoth?) and released the waters of the Penobscot River. For example, a monster frog, *Aglebemu*, was monopolizing the world's water and would allow humans to have none. Gluskabe seized Aglebemu and squeezed him, making him small, with bulging eyes and a crooked back. No longer powerful, he hides in swamps and ponds, still mumbling, "Give 'em

This large wooden statue is a depiction of Gluskabe, the great transformer/trickster, as imagined by sculptor Peter Toth. It stands by the Bar Harbor Road on Mount Desert Island. *Photo by author.*

none." Meanwhile, Gluskabe released the waters, and some people were so thirsty that they dove right in and were transformed into fish and other aquatic creatures.

Many features of animals and the landscape are ascribed to the transforming actions of Gluskabe; skunk smells bad because Gluskabe smeared the sludge from his pipe on him as punishment for envy, and sweet grass smells good because it was touched by the breath of Gluskabe. His overturned cook pot can be seen on Moosehead Lake as Mount Kineo; on the coast, it is said his stone canoe can be seen near Castine, where he beached it to chase a moose. The moose's hindquarters can be seen on the shore between Harborside and Cape Rosier (in the form of a rock best viewed at half tide), and the animal's entrails, which he threw over the cape, appear as a streak of white quartz on Islesboro, in a bluff between Ryder's Cove and the point below. The moose's liver is now a ledge (Thrumcap Ledge on modern charts) near the head of Eggemoggin Reach in Penobscot Bay and served as a marker for two canoe portage routes across Cape Rosier.

The traditional world of the Etchemins was alive, and every living thing had its own distinctive power. The earth was "our grandmother," the producer of all life when warmed by the sun. The all-important birch

Mount Kineo on Moosehead Lake in Maine. In one version of a Gluskabe tale, it is his overturned cook pot. In another, it is the body of a moose he killed. For thousands of years, the mountain was a major source of stone used to make a variety of stone tools. *Courtesy John G. Crock.*

trees would "shed their blankets (bark) to give people shelter" in the form of houses. The Creator had a concern for the animals and plants, and even today when a Penobscot harvests the game animals and medicinal plants that are needed, he or she does so with care and respect, observing well-established procedures. The bones of beaver, muskrat and waterfowl were returned to the water with a request that they continue their species. When drinking from a spring, an offering of tobacco was left for the resident spirit. Before eating, a grease offering was made on the fire to thank the Creator of the four-leggeds. All waste of food was avoided so as not to offend this being. Medicinal plants were gathered with care to take only one of a "family" of colony plants and to shake the seeds of other plants into the hole made by pulling out the roots.

Of the creatures of the air, the thunders with their great power were friendly to humans, but the wind bird was considered dangerous. One of the Gluskabe stories has him abating strong winds by tying the wings of the giant wind bird. This created a world with no wind at all, causing the air to become hot and hard to breathe and the water to grow dirty and smelly. Having gone from one extreme of constant high winds to the other of no wind at all, Gluskabe went back, freed one wing, leaving the other one tied, which allowed for the winds we experience today. Thus was the proper balance achieved. *Pmola*, the spirit of Mount Katahdin, was a flying creature of immense power who could alter his size at will. He was sometimes described as propelling himself with a bull roarer (a noisemaker at the end of a line) in each hand. Though potentially dangerous, Pmola could be called to a hunter's assistance. Still, Indians avoided climbing above the tree line.

In general, various underwater creatures are people's natural enemies. Among these is an underwater monster, *Wiwiliamecq*, with whom the famed nineteenth-century shaman John Neptune once did battle in Boyden's Lake in Washington County. The waters of this lake today are said to be still riled up from the fight. Another is *Pskedemus*, a spirit that can be heard calling from swamps and may lure children into swamps from which they will not return. This particular tale demonstrates how stories were used to influence children's behavior, teaching as they entertain.

The *Manôgemassak* are a race of little people who live under water in the rivers. They are shy but not ill-natured, have thin faces like an axe blade and speak their own language in squeaky voices. When surprised by a human being, they submerge in their stone canoes and disappear. Stories about underwater creatures were not told until they were safely frozen beneath the ice, when they cannot hear the stories and so gain power from them.

A world in which not only animals and plants but also even rocks might be alive contains great potential for the appearance of a variety of beings even beyond the ones just described. Some are associated with particular places that are in some way special. One such place was on the coast at Machias. So special was the power of this place that people came here on vision quests, to establish contact with some spirit being. In a state of trance or in a dream, a spirit would appear to the supplicant. Some who experienced such visions at this sacred place recorded them afterward, in the form of images inscribed in the ledges through which the spirits traveled from the "other" world. The first of these images were inscribed about 3,000 years ago, and others were added continuously up to 380 years ago. As late as the 1790s, there are reports of seasonal gatherings here with more than one hundred canoes and sounds of drumming going on through the night. The site remains important today to the Passamaquoddy people.

One of the Machias petroglyphs, in this case a depiction of a visionary shaman invested with his spirit helper (implied by his empty body). This is one of the older images, made about two thousand years ago. *Courtesy Mark Heddon.*

ETCHEMIN SHAMANISM

Potentially, anyone had the ability to contact the supernatural world. This stemmed from the Etchemin concept of self. Each person was thought to be made up of two parts: the body and what might be called an inner self. This latter was dependent on the body yet was able to disengage and have "out of body" experiences. Detached from the body, it could travel about, interact with others and participate in various activities, as was thought to happen in dreams. There was, however, a danger; if the inner self returned to the body before too much time passed, all was well. But if it did not, the individual would sicken and, should the inner self not return at all, die. Since every individual could potentially wield supernatural powers, with which every living thing was endowed, it was thought possible for anyone's inner self to be lured away from the body by someone else, the result being sickness or eventual death.

These characteristics of the self are displayed most vividly in the case of shamans, usually (but not exclusively) men whose powers were greater than those of most people, enabling them to impose their will on the spirit world. Shamans enjoyed the reputation of being able to see things taking place afar and foretell the future. They were also believed to possess the ability to locate game through divination, perhaps by heating the shoulder blade of a deer or moose over a fire and interpreting the cracks and smudges as a map of the hunting territory. They also effected certain cures of ailments by virtue of their mental powers. Generally, these involved ailments regarded as extraordinary because they did not respond to ordinary herbal medicine. Finally, they were thought to be able to walk so powerfully that their feet sank into the very rock, and because their sexual appetites were regarded as above normal, shamans were likely to keep multiple wives.

Although a shaman was born with more than the ordinary amount of supernatural power, that power had to be cultivated to be effective. Crucial for this was success in gaining power over an animal helper. Although many men commonly sought such a helper, a shaman was more skilled at its use. A shaman was able to transfer his inner self into the animal's body at will, his own body remaining inert for the duration. This was not without danger, however, for if the animal was killed at this time, the shaman also died. But then, the job of killing was complicated by the shaman's ability to shape-shift; that is, transform into something else, such as a bird or fleet-footed animal, and get away. A shaman might also send his animal helper off to run errands without actually transferring his inner self to it. Animals reputed to have served as shaman's helpers include the bear, beaver, various birds, dogs, eel, otter and porcupine. An especially powerful shaman could have more than one helper; one famous Penobscot shaman had seven. The way to gain control over an animal helper was to go alone into the woods and, in a state of trance, sing for it to appear. The first animal seen in one's vision that could be stroked was by that bound to the shaman's service. From then on, its flesh was taboo to the shaman.

An Etchemin shaman also derived power from his drum, which gave him the ability to communicate with the spirit world. One Passamaquoddy put it this way: "Storms hearken to the sound of my drum…The wood spirit ceases chopping to listen to my drum…Lightning, thunder, storms, gale, forest, water spirit, whirlwind, spirit of the night and air are gathered together and are listening to my drum."

In northern New England and on up into Labrador, the shaman's drum was a wooden hoop with a head of green deerskin. Over this were two rawhide strings that produced a buzzing sound, thought to represent singing.

Along with his drum, the shaman had his cedar flute. This conveyed the power to call game, lure enemies and attract women. Finally, there was the shaman's ability to perform tricks. Normally, he was adept at fooling people with sleight of hand, ventriloquism and similar arts. This sort of thing is typical of shamanism, wherever found, and is one reason why nonbelievers often regard practitioners as charlatans. The fact is that a shaman is usually quite sincere about the job and regards his ability to perform tricks as one more proof of his superior power, much as the Puritans in late seventeenth-century Massachusetts believed that commercial success was a measure of God's favor.

The Etchemin way of life, with roots extending back several thousand years, was a remarkably successful one. Had it not been, it could not have survived over so long a period. In today's world, the pace of change is such that it is all too easy to regard long periods of relative cultural stability as a sign of stagnation or lack of progress. To do so, however, is not justified, as one culture cannot be objectively evaluated by another's values. Neither is it correct to conclude that a people such as the Etchemins and their ancestors lacked the leisure time that would have permitted cultural elaboration. In fact, there now exists a large body of evidence that shows quite clearly that foraging people, as a rule, have more leisure time available to them than do most people who grow their own food. The likelihood is that at the start of the seventeenth century, Etchemins probably had more leisure time, a better diet, a slightly longer life expectancy and less violence in their lives than did most people then living in Europe. Nor should we forget that the Europeans who came to North America to live owed their very survival to knowledge gained from the native inhabitants.

To conclude, by developing a sustainable way of life that allowed people to utilize the environment to their advantage, Etchemins secured their survival and saw to the reasonable satisfaction of their needs as they themselves perceived them. Such are the only objective criteria by which the success or failure of a culture may be judged.

Chapter 3
Defending the Homeland

When Champlain sailed along the Etchemin Coast in 1604, he encountered a people who had never seen a European before. They had, of course, heard about them; after all, the Mi'kmaqs, with whom they regularly interacted, had been dealing with these strangers since early in the sixteenth century. Seeing them in the flesh, however, was something else altogether. As Champlain noted at his meeting with Bashaba at Kadesquit (Kenduskeag, Bangor), the natives "greatly enjoyed looking at us, for it was the first time that they had seen Christians" (meaning Europeans). Generally, the French had a favorable opinion of Indians, and Bashaba in particular, whom Jesuits in 1611 described as "a man of great discretion and prudence." Champlain regarded Indians, in general, as equal in intelligence and judgment to Europeans, and he was impressed by their qualities of mind. His fellow Frenchman Mark Lescarbot had similar admiration, and wrote, "They have courage, fidelity, generosity, and humanity, and their hospitality is so innate and so praiseworthy that they receive among them every man who is not an enemy. They are not simpletons."

The French were impressed as well by the physical appearance of the Indians. Champlain spoke of their straight limbs, strong muscles, teeth that were perfectly straight and white and their health, which seemed better than that of Europeans. "All these people are well proportioned in body, without deformity," he observed. "They are agile, and the women are well shaped, filled out and plump, and of a swarthy color."

Champlain's 1607 map of the Gulf of Maine. Note the Indian villages shown on the Saint John, Saint Croix, Union, Penobscot (at the Kenduskeag) and Kennebec Rivers. *Courtesy Library of Congress Map Collections: http://hdl.loc.gov/loc.gmd/g3321p.np000002.*

Much as Indians admired European technology, such as guns, iron axes and brass and iron kettles, they were not impressed by Europeans themselves. The Mi'kmaqs, for example, considered them "as physically inferior, as weak and unfitted to stand up to the rigors of arduous canoe journeys, hunting expeditions, and forest warfare." Often looking down on the Europeans, they "found them ugly, especially because of their excessive hairiness, and their frequent deformities and infirmities. Furthermore," as one writer noted, "[Mi'kmaqs] are as proud as can be...[and] considered the French less intelligent than they."

The Jesuit priest Pierre Biard, who met with Bashaba and a large contingent of Etchemins in 1611, wrote that they

> *conclude generally that they are superior to all Christians...They regard themselves as much richer than we are...they consider themselves better than the French: "for," they say "you're always fighting and quarreling among yourselves: we live peaceably. You are envious and are all the time slandering each other; you are thieves and deceivers; you are covetous, and are neither generous nor kind; as for us, if we have a morsel of bread we share it with our neighbor." They are saying these and like things continually.*

76

THE HOSTILITIES BEGIN

Very quickly, the Etchemins began trading with the French, exchanging beaver and other pelts for desirable kettles, guns and axes, among other things. The French, for their part, saw the opportunity to profit, as beaver skins were in high demand in Europe. Felt hats made from beaver fur were all the rage on that continent, but the native animals were all but exterminated. The French were smart enough to realize that the successful fur trade depended on good relations with the Indians. The natives, for their part, were happy to have direct access to the foreigners' material goods and not have to deal with Mi'kmaq middlemen. They were also quick to see that they could benefit in another way by making use of the newcomers in their escalating troubles with Tarrentine raiders.

For a long time, the two parties got along well. The French may not have realized it, but for the Indians, trade was as much a diplomatic as an economic activity. It signaled good intentions on the part of those so engaged. Moreover, the exchange of weapons was an essential part of native protocol. So the French willingness to supply guns and ammunition, as well as to service the weapons, helped cement the relationship between the two sides. The Indians, for their part, quickly recognized the superiority of firearms for hunting and so abandoned their bows and arrows. Thus began a loss of self-sufficiency as they became increasingly dependent on Europeans for supplies.

Amicable relations with the French were further strengthened by intermarriage between the two groups. Unfortunately, this growing harmony was interrupted in 1605 by the arrival of the English captain George Weymouth, who anchored his vessel off Allen Island at the western entrance to Penobscot Bay. Weymouth not only rebuffed diplomatic overtures from Bashaba, an ominous sign by itself, but he also kidnapped five of the local Indians, including Chief Tahánedo of Pemaquid. A year later, after a sojourn on one of the manorial estates of Sir John Popham, lord chief justice of England, Tahánedo was enlisted to guide the vessel piloted by Martin Pring along the Maine coast to the lower Kennebec. Once there, he returned to his band ranging in the Pemaquid and Muscongus Bay area. A second captive, Skidwarres, returned in 1607 with a party of English intent on establishing a colony on the lower Kennebec. Stopping off on the way at Pemaquid, there was a meeting with Tahánedo and his band, in which the Etchemins showed themselves to be quite wary of the English. For his part, Skidwarres took advantage of the opportunity to disappear into the woods with Tahánedo's people, keeping his distance thereafter from the English.

This statue of an Indian with food stands beside the trail in Saint Croix Island National Park, on the mainland opposite the island. *Courtesy John M. Roberts.*

As for the other three captives, one returned either with Taháñedo or Skidwarres. The other two were on another vessel, bound for the colony-to-be on the Kennebec, that had the misfortune of being captured by a Spanish vessel. One of these two Etchemins managed to escape and, after a nine-year absence, returned to his homeland. The other died in captivity.

Despite the capture of one ship, the English proceeded with their plans, establishing the Popham colony in the district of Etchemin sagamo Sebora (like Taháñedo, one of Bashaba's sub-chiefs in the Mawooshen Confederacy). There, the colony's commander, Sir George Popham, was visited by various Abenaki and Etchemin sagamos hoping for assistance in their troubles with Tarrentine raiders. In this, however, they were disappointed. Native protocol would have required Popham to visit Bashaba at his headquarters to pay proper respect to the grand chief of the country in which they proposed to settle. This he refused to do, despite entreaties from the local chiefs. Relations with the Indians soured as the year wore on, as according to the Jesuit Pierre Biard: "They [the colonists] drove the savages away without ceremony; they beat, maltreated, and misused them outrageously."

Defending the Homeland

One reported outrage concerned a group of natives who were enticed into the English fort under pretense of trade. "Causing them to take the drags of a loaded cannon, [the English] fired off the piece when the Indians were in line, and blew them to atoms."

Not surprisingly, the Popham colony failed, but troubles with the English were far from over. In 1609, the *Half Moon*, a Dutch vessel commanded by Henry Hudson, entered the Gulf of Maine. Somewhere at either Mount Desert Island or the western shore of Penobscot Bay, Hudson had a surprise meeting with "two French shallops full of the country people," probably Eastern Etchemins or Mi'kmaqs. After a week of trading, Hudson and his crew made an unprovoked attack on the Indians where they were camped, seized all of their belongings, as well as one of their shallops, and then departed. Since Hudson and half his crew spoke English, this would have been seen as yet another act of violence by these foreigners. Clearly, these people were not to be trusted!

More trouble followed. In 1611, Captain Edward Harlow kidnapped three Indians on Monhegan Island. One managed to escape, but the other two, with five others captured off Cape Cod, were transported to England. By contrast, in that same year, the French fur trader Biencourt and Jesuit

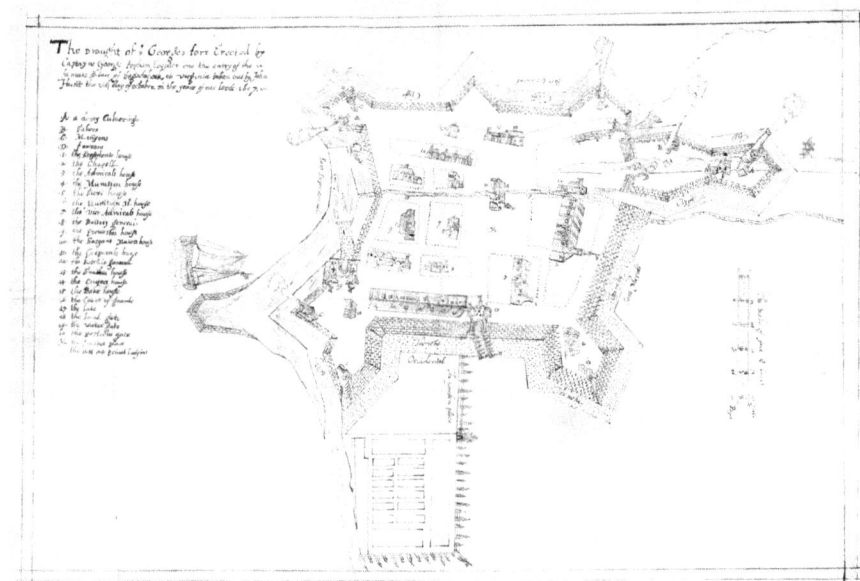

Map of Fort St. George made by a member of the colonizing expedition. This was the first attempt by the English to establish themselves in the Etchemin homeland. *Courtesy Maine Historical Society.*

priest Biard were welcomed by Bashaba and three hundred Etchemins at their seasonal encampment on the Bagaduce River (called *chiboctous* by the Etchemins, for the large upriver tidal bays), near where it runs into Penobscot Bay. Two years later, Father Biard was invited by Chief Asticou and his Etchemin band to establish a mission settlement on Mount Desert Island's Somes Sound, but within months, this was attacked and destroyed by the British captain Samuel Argall. A year later, Captain John Smith sailed into Penobscot Bay, with Tahánedo on board as a guide. Here he did well trading with the local inhabitants, although he referred to these meetings dismissively as "silly encounters." At least he did not kidnap anyone, though one of his companion captains, Thomas Hunt, seized several Indians on Monhegan Island. These, with others captured elsewhere (including Squanto, who was later to aid the Plymouth colonists), were sold to Spanish slave traders.

By this time, Mawooshen had become a war zone. Already, Tarrentines had been raiding as far south as Saco Bay and would extend their activities even as far south as Cape Cod. In western Etchemin country, they gained control of the lands and islands east of Penobscot Bay and, in 1615, raided Bashaba's village at Kadesquit, killing him and several of his followers. Although he was succeeded as grand chief by Asticou of the Frenchman Bay area, the Mawooshen Alliance was thrown into turmoil. The final blow was the Great Dying, caused by a disease introduced from Europe, which began in 1616. The specific disease, which killed off up to 90 percent of native populations, has never been adequately diagnosed. What is known is that the poor sanitary conditions in most European communities created optimal conditions for the incubation of such afflictions as bubonic and pneumonic plague, chickenpox, cholera, diphtheria, dysentery, influenza, measles, scarlet fever, smallpox, tuberculosis, typhus, typhoid and whooping cough. Because Europeans had been living with these for centuries, they acquired a certain resistance, if not outright immunity, to them. In the Americas, however, these diseases were absent until they were brought over, unwittingly, by travelers from Europe. Hence, Americans lacked all resistance to them and succumbed in large numbers, even as the newcomers did not.

In the midst of all this disease, death and political turmoil, the Frenchman Claude de La Tour established a trading post at Pentagöet (from the Etchemin word *pentagwet*, meaning "at the falls," the name of the lower narrows of the Bagaduce River, a short distance upstream from Castine). A friend of the Mi'kmaq, de la Tour was ousted by colonists from Plymouth in 1629, who renamed the place Penobscote (from *penapskot*, "at the descending rock," referring to Dice's Head at Castine, an important landmark for canoeists). The pilgrims, in turn, were ousted in 1635, by which time England had formally given up claims to lands from Penobscot Bay to Cape Breton. The new governor of Acadia, Charles d'Aulney, promptly enlarged and fortified the trading post into Fort Pentagöet.

With the end of the Great Dying in 1618, surviving Etchemins began to regroup, being joined by some of their Abenaki allies from the old Mawooshen Confederacy. By the end of the 1630s, the power of the Mi'kmaqs and their Eastern Etchemin allies was on the wane, as access to guns became more widespread. As one English observer noted: "He is a poor Indian that is not master of two guns, which they purchase of the French, and powder and shot."

From the first, the Indians recognized the superiority of flintlock, as opposed to matchlock guns, some fifty years ahead of the English colonists. With flintlocks, loading was simpler and quicker, and the guns were quicker and easier to fire. Furthermore, a lighted match was not needed in advance of firing. As early as 1607, Indians knew of this last disadvantage of matchlocks, as revealed by an account of a group that came aboard an English shallop: "One of the Indians came into the shallop and taking the firebrand, which one of our company held in his hand there to light the matches, as if he

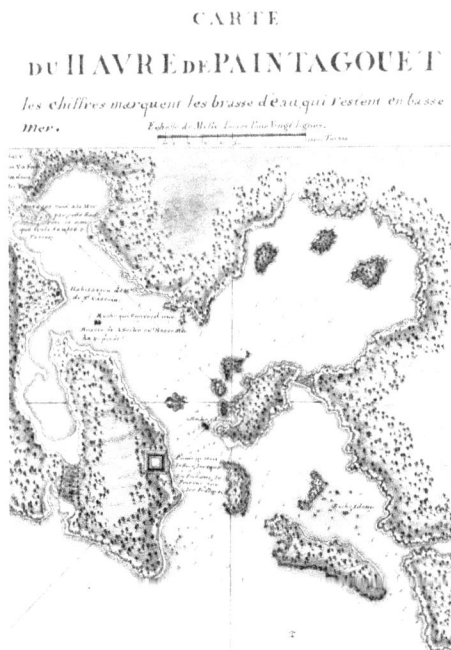

CARTE

DU HAVRE DE PAINTAGOUET

les chiffres marquent les brasse d'eau qui restent en basse mer.

This 1688 map of Pentagöet Harbor at the mouth of the Bagaduce River shows Saint-Castin's habitation on the point above the Castine peninsula (left). At the upper left is Pentagwet, the first narrows of the Bagaduce, from which comes the name Pentagöet. *Courtesy Aix-en-Provence (Côte du document). Tous droits reserves.*

would light a pipe of tobacco, and as soon as he [the Indian] had gotten it into his hand he presently threw it into the water."

By doing so, the English crew was effectively rendered harmless.

RESISTING THE ENGLISH

At the same time that the Mi'kmaqs were losing their advantage in the indigenous arms race, the threat from the English and their Indian allies, the Iroquois (traditional enemies of the Abenakis and Etchemins), was on the increase. In 1654, the English again drove the French from Pentagöet as well as from Forte Sainte-Marie on the lower St. John River and Port Royal in Nova Scotia. One would have thought that with the region under English control, Iroquois raids would be restrained. The Abenakis of Norridgewock, a village on the Kennebec, evidently thought they would be safe in 1662, when a group of one hundred, mostly women and children, traveled to Fort Pentagöet seeking protection at this stronghold. To their dismay, they found out otherwise and were captured there by an Iroquois raiding party.

Despite the English takeover, skirmishes continued all along the coast, including one not far from Pentagöet, where Indians seized an English fishing vessel, burning it and killing the crew. Perhaps this was in retaliation for the failure to protect the Abenakis at the fort. Whatever the case, the English retaliated by destroying a nearby village on Walker's Pond (source of the Bagaduce River), from which a portage led to the site of the vessel's seizure. Most of the villagers seem to have survived the destruction and relocated their village to the upper end of the pond, at the head of the portage.

This relocated village was the headquarters of the sagamo who would become prominent in succeeding decades as a worthy successor to Bashaba, from whom (along with Asticou) he was descended. This was Madockawando, whose name has been variously translated as "Wonder Worker" or "Strong Spirit Power." Both reflect a reputation for great supernatural powers as a shaman. He seems to have been a particularly charismatic leader who rose to power by building up wealth through the fur trade, the major trading post being just downstream at Pentagöet, near the mouth of the Bagaduce, the source of which is Walker's Pond. Added status would have come from his prowess as a war chief and shaman, not to mention his relationship to his famous Etchemin forbear. Even more prestige came from his marriage to a Kennebec Abenaki woman, his sister's marriage to a Kennebec man and a fictive relationship to the Abenaki headman of a village at the confluence of the Kennebec and the Sebasticook Rivers. This location was on a major canoe route that, via a portage from the Sebasticook to the Kenduskeag, gave access to the Penobscot. Thus, Madockawando was able to extend his influence far beyond his immediate territory, which included Frenchman Bay on the east, Penobscot Bay on the west and the river itself. Before his life ended, he was able to revive the old Mawooshen alliance, being recognized by other sagamos along the coast as grand chief. What's more, he played an important role in expanding the old alliance to include its former enemies, the Mi'kmaqs and Eastern Etchemins, laying the basis for the Wabanaki Confederacy.

In 1667, a new treaty restored French control of Etchemin country from the Bay of Fundy to somewhere around Muscongus Bay. From there to the west and south, the English continued to hold sway. Not until 1670, however, were French troops able to repossess Fort Pentagöet. Among the French was a young officer: Jean-Vincent d'Abbedie, who would become the Baron de Saint-Castin. Through marriage to two of Madockawando's daughters, he would go on to produce several métis children. For his part, Madockawando saw these marriages as a way to extend his influence to the French. Both Saint-Castin and his sons, who became war chiefs and fur traders, would go on to play important roles in Etchemin country. Evidently, Jean-Vincent wasted no time getting to know Madockawando and his family, as Jean-Vincent's first daughter was born within a year of his arrival.

One of the first acts of the new governor of Acadia, the Chevalier de Grandfontaine, was to commission a map of his domains along the Maine coast. Probably drawn by Saint-Castin, it shows his father-in-law Madockawando's fortified lodge at the head of Walker's Pond, a strategic position. Located on an important portage in a region with abundant resources, it was close enough to a major shipping lane (Eggemoggin Reach) to be aware of what vessels were passing but far enough from the coast to be out of sight of potentially hostile ships. A second fortified lodge is shown on Grandfontaine's map upstream on the Penobscot River at Veazie Falls, near the mouth of Eaton Brook. Just as his illustrious predecessor, Bashaba, maintained a second seasonal village on the Bagaduce, so may Madockawando have maintained one upriver, not far from where Bashaba once had his headquarters. Moreover, Eaton Brook used to be accessible by canoe to within two miles of the important Union River. By Indian standards, this is not a long portage, and they used this route to access the waters surrounding Mount Desert Island.

When the French resumed control of Acadia, there were no more than about 500 Europeans in all of this region that ran from Muscongus Bay to Cape Breton. By contrast, there were around 750 Etchemins still living in their country, with some 1,750 Mi'kmaqs to the north. The Etchemins still

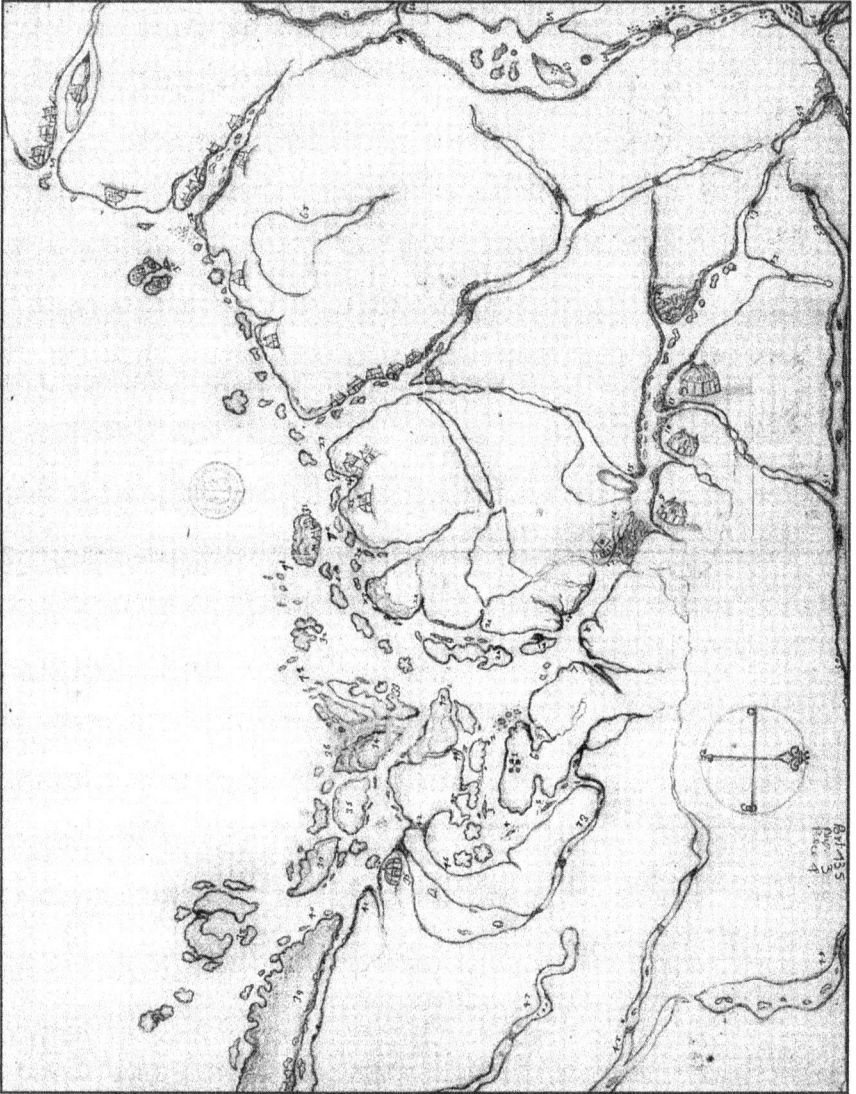

Grandfontain's 1671 map of the coast, from Mount Desert Island to the Kennebec and beyond. Note that on the east may be seen Madockawando's fort at the head of Walker's Pond. Upriver, the fort numbered nine may also have been his. *Courtesy Document conserve aux Archives Nationals, Paris. Cliché Atelier Photographique des Archives Nationals.*

retained their independence, although they had to constantly keep a wary eye out for English and Iroquoian enemies. As much as possible, they made use of canoe routes that kept them out of sight of enemy vessels. South from Pemaquid, there were few Etchemins, being replaced by Abenakis who were moving east in response to pressures from expanding populations in the New England colonies. These Abenakis lived under trying circumstances, as the English allowed their livestock to ruin native cornfields, plied the natives with alcohol to get them to deed land to the colonists and generally treated them in a patronizing way at best but more often with contempt. All too often, Indians were seen as a source of amusement and were given demeaning nicknames derived from burlesques and ribald celebrations. A prime example is that conferred upon the Abenaki sagamo Rawandagon, whom the English called Robin Hood, not for the hero of Sherwood Forest, but for a character in the bawdy May Fair festivals of England. Clearly, it was meant as an insult.

Despite the French presence, skirmishes continued along the Etchemin coast. In 1674, Dutch raiders destroyed Fort Pentagöet, which was never rebuilt. Saint-Castin, however, remained at his trading post, which was located upstream from the fort. The location was a good one, at the convergence of at least seven canoe routes going east, north and west, and it could not be seen from vessels on Penobscot Bay. Madockawando and his Etchemins, as well as Abenakis, would gather here periodically, as in the mid-1680s, when a French account recorded 160 Indians in thirty-two bark dwellings surrounding St. Castin's house. He remained here until 1701, when he returned to France to deal with matters of inheritance.

Things came to a head in 1675, when the Indians of southern New England launched a desperate uprising to preserve what was left of their freedoms in the face of English provocations. To the north, Abenakis and Etchemins watched as the colonists effectively destroyed their southern neighbors. The Abenakis were particularly affected, as refugees fled north to escape the extermination of their peoples. At the same time, colonists in their region were pressuring the Abenakis to disarm and, in fact, give up their last vestiges of independence. As a consequence, many fled to the country of their old Mawooshen allies, the Etchemins, east of Pemaquid. For their part, the Etchemins tried to remain neutral in the face of all this upheaval. Then, in 1675, William Waldron, of New Hampshire, kidnapped fifteen natives off Machias under pretext of trading with them, selling them into slavery in the Azores. This act so outraged Madockawando and his people that it was impossible to remain neutral. Reviving the old Mawooshen alliance, they embarked on all-out warfare with the English. Saint-Castin played a key role in this as provider of guns and ammunition, enabling the Indians to achieve a number of successes. But they suffered setbacks as well. For example, in February 1677, a number of Indians with some English captives arrived at Pemaquid to negotiate peace. After negotiating the release of the captives, the English turned without warning and proceeded to kill as many Indians as they could. One of those killed was the Abenaki husband of Madockawando's sister, and she herself was taken prisoner.

In addition to the violence, the disruption of normal subsistence activities took its toll. So, too, did diseases, as another round of epidemic struck in the winter of 1675–76. Finally, in late summer 1677, Madockawando traveled to Pemaquid to negotiate peace with the English. Joined by other Abenaki chiefs from the west, peace was officially declared. In the treaty, English colonial authorities recognized Indian sovereignty over lands east of Pemaquid.

For a decade, relations between the English and Madockawando's people were strained at best. Iroquois aggression and colonial expansion from New England continued to upset the Indians, who sought strength through expanded alliance with the Eastern Etchemins and Mi'kmaqs in what would be known as the Wabanaki Confederacy. Instituting regular formal meetings at their council fires, they (like the Iroquois) began using wampum belts in their diplomacy. Then, in 1688, violence erupted again into full-scale war.

Even before this new conflict, the English had decided to assert territorial claims to the region between the St. George and St. Croix Rivers. Then, in 1688, New England's governor, Andros, pillaged Saint-Castin's trading post. For their part, the French, in 1687, sent a number of Abenaki refugees who had fled to Canadian mission villages to *Panawamské*, "opening out upon a ledgy place," today's Indian Island at Old Town. A practice going back before the arrival of Europeans was the adoption of outsiders into Indian communities, and in the tense situation that then existed, these reinforcements were generally welcomed.

The pillaging of Saint-Castin's establishment, coupled with other acts of violence against Abenakis, caused Wabanaki warriors to retaliate, forcing the English evacuation of all of their settlements east of the Kennebec. Joining the Wabanaki war party were French officers and soldiers, who had their own quarrel with the English. The English, of course, retaliated, raiding all along the coast from the Bay of Chaleur to the Penobscot. Among the casualties was the Acadian capital Port Royal and the capture of one of Saint-Castin's daughters, who was taken as a hostage to Boston.

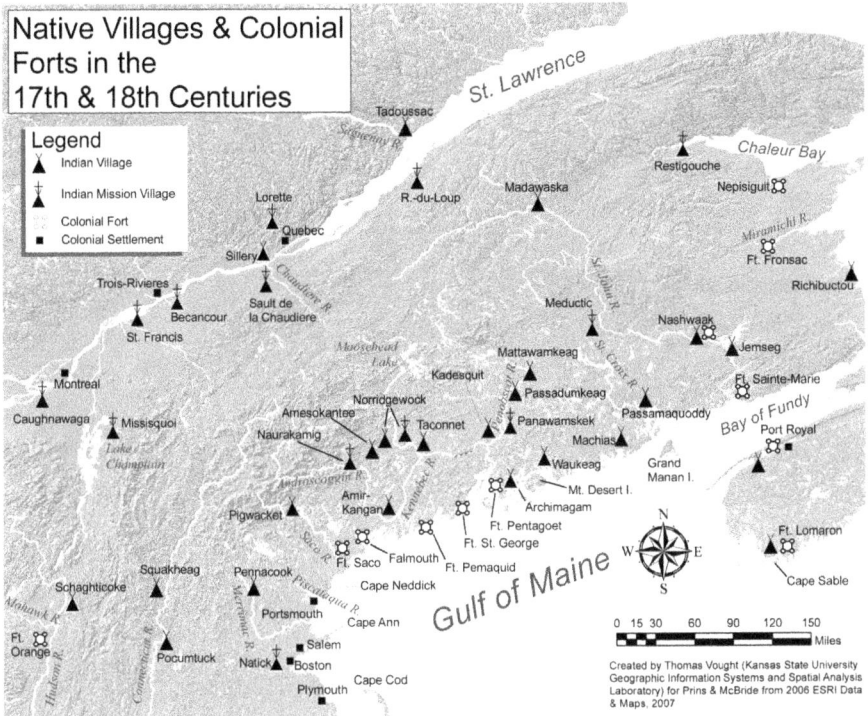

Native villages and colonial forts in the seventeenth and eighteenth centuries. *Prins and McBride 2007: 190. Courtesy Harald E.L. Prins.*

With the fall of Port Royal, the French commander of Acadian forces moved to the Saint John River. Having lived in Mi'kmaq country, he began using their name for neighboring groups: Maliseets for Etchemins and Canibas for Abenakis. In 1694, the "Maliseets" were reportedly still in place between the Saint John and the Penobscot Rivers, but "at Pentagöet, among the Malicites [Etchemins] are many Canibas [Abenaki] Indians." Besides Pentagöet, bands were at the head of Frenchman Bay, Machias, Passamaquoddy Bay and the Saint John Valley. The farther east one went, the fewer Abenakis there were among the Etchemins.

Even in the face of constant attacks by English colonial raiders, the Etchemins managed to prevent them from establishing any settlements. At Pemaquid, however, the English returned in 1692 and built a large stone fort, the strongest garrison on the Atlantic seaboard. A year later, Madockawando and allied Wabanaki chiefs went there to attend a peace meeting with Sir William Phips, governor of Massachusetts Bay. Though

Modern reconstruction of Fort William Henry, the English stronghold at Pemaquid. In 1693, Madockawando and twelve other chiefs concluded a peace treaty with New England's governor here. Three years later, a combined French and Indian force captured the fort. *Photo by the author.*

reluctant, Madockawando supported the treaty, perhaps in part to secure the release of his granddaughter, Saint-Castin's daughter, who had been captured three years earlier. Not all chiefs agreed to peace, however, and encouraged by the French, they continued to wage guerrilla war.

By the summer of 1696, French warships left the Saint John River and sailed for Pentagöet and Saint-Castin's habitation, where they were joined by some 250 Wabanaki warriors. Madockawando, having yielded to pressures to again go on the warpath, was among them. After the appropriate feasting and deliberation, twenty-five French marines and the Wabanakis under Saint-Castin's command sailed for Pemaquid, determined to take the fort down. There, Saint-Castin persuaded the fort's commander to surrender. The English were promised safe passage to Boston, the fort was demolished, its guns and ammunition distributed to the Indians and the artillery taken aboard the French ships.

Naturally, all of this triggered a response, and a massive English force set sail from Massachusetts Bay. Following a tip, the fleet voyaged up the Penobscot River expecting to find the enemy. In this they failed, so they went next to Naskeag (from the *Kwinaskeag* "long point of land") on Blue Hill Bay. Here they found abandoned houses and cornfields, with similar results on nearby Deer Isle. From there, they went on to Mount Desert, used as a staging area for raids by the Indians, but again all for naught.

Defending the Homeland

The following season, a combined force of Maliseets (Etchemins) and Mi'kmaqs departed from Meductic, an Etchemin village on the Saint John River, traveling interior waterways to Pentagöet. From there, they resumed their guerrilla raids. Finally, in 1697, the French and English resolved their differences in Europe, with this news reaching the French in the Saint John Valley a year later. In 1699, the chiefs representing the Wabanaki Confederacy signed their own treaty with the English.

An uneasy peace followed, lasting a mere five years. During this time, an effort by the governor of New England to assert sovereignty over those Abenakis still present in the Kennebec Valley was firmly resisted. They would agree to a "league of friendship," but nothing more. As for Madockawando, he died in 1698 at Meductic, a victim of yet another epidemic, this one probably brought by French sailors from the Caribbean. Hundreds of others died as well. At the time of his death, Madockawando was living at Meductic, rather than his traditional home, as a consequence of the division in the preceding conflict between those who preferred negotiation and Abenakis who wished to press on with the fight. Three years after Madockawando's death, Saint-Castin left for France, to straighten out affairs of his estate. There he died in 1607. His métis sons, however, including the one who inherited his title, stayed in the Penobscot Bay region and played prominent roles as war chiefs in the new conflicts that erupted in 1703.

Not all Wabanakis were in favor of war in 1703, but the French were already embroiled in one with the English in Europe, and the French in Canada finally persuaded the Indians to join in. The thing that tipped the balance was an English privateer who raided the home of Saint-Castin's daughter Brigitte and her husband, Philippe Meunier, at Naskeag, at the entrance to Blue Hill Bay. Here, they killed Philippe, raped Brigitte and probably killed her as well. This so outraged the Indians that a large contingent raided Casco and Wells, prompting Massachusetts to declare total war on the Wabanakis. Other sons and daughters of Saint-Castin caught up in these new hostilities were his older daughter, Claire, and his eldest son, Bernard-Anselm, who was to inherit the title of "Baron" when his father died. Claire and her children were captured somewhere on Penobscot Bay and were held in Boston until the war's end, later going to live on Mount Desert Island. Bernard became a war chief, conducting guerrilla actions against the English at Port Royal. Meanwhile, English forces systematically ransacked Wabanaki villages all along the coast. Finally, in 1710, Port Royal fell to the English, with all of the Wabanaki coast now in their possession.

The year 1713 brought about a new interval of uneasy peace. With the French gone and upwards of 150,000 colonial settlers in New England, some of whom were casting covetous eyes on lands east of Pemaquid, Wabanakis had reason for concern. This was in spite of explicit acknowledgment of their aboriginal rights. At the same time that they felt pressures from developers, fishermen increasingly interfered with traditional subsistence activities along the coast. Then, in 1721, the English kidnapped Joseph d'Abbedie, another of Saint-Castin's sons who, with younger brother Barenos, was running the family fur-trading business at the old homestead at Pentagöet. Joseph succeeded to Bernard-Anselm's position as fur trader and war chief following his brother's departure with his family in 1714 to claim his baronial inheritance. Prior to Joseph's capture, a group of Wabanakis—perhaps relatives of Joseph and Barenos—captured some Massachusetts fishermen, probably in Fox Island Thorofare (between North Haven and Vinalhaven in Penobscot Bay). After Joseph's return in 1722, a New England sloop that put into Pentagöet Harbor was seized, and by 1723, full-scale warfare had resumed. Part of the problem was the construction of forts at the St. George River, just west of Penobscot Bay, and at Richmond, on the lower Kennebec, a worrisome expansion of English territory.

During this new hot war, called Dummer's War (after the Massachusetts governor) or Lovewell's War (after a southern Maine militia captain), colonial forces burned the settlement at Panawamské (Indian Island), where they found

This 1856 engraving depicts the destruction of Norridgewock, an Abenaki village on the Kennebec, and the death of the French priest there. Some of those who escaped the massacre fled east into Penobscot country. *Courtesy Maine Historical Society.*

twenty-three "well-finished wigwams," and destroyed Norridgewock on the upper Kennebec. Both were genocidal attacks, designed to kill everyone, but the village on the Penobscot was deserted at the time. At Norridgewock, however, people were present, and many were killed, including women, children and the French mission priest, who was scalped. Those who were able to fled, though many drowned in the attempt. Some, however, made it to mission villages in Canada, others to the Penobscot, including "One-Arm Nicola," who lost half his right forearm in the conflict. His descendant, Joseph Nicolar, would later be a representative to the Maine legislature and author of an important book, *The Life and Traditions of the Red Man*.

Along the coast, the English continued to harass natives wherever they encountered them. By 1725, a bounty on Indian scalps was offered: £100 for each male above the age of twelve and, for others, "the highest premium the law allows." Meanwhile, Wabanakis operating out of Mount Dessert Island carried on guerrilla tactics seriously interfering with fishing vessels, as when Joseph d'Abbedie and several Indians captured nine vessels off the Fox Islands in 1724. They made good use of them, causing colonial authorities to complain that Indians "infest the eastern coast in the schooner [actually, several] by them taken from English."

By the fall of 1725, it was becoming evident to the Wabanakis that, without direct French military support, they were too few in number to stand up to the forces of New England. The Penobscots (as the descendants of the old Mawooshen Confederacy were now called) agreed to lay down their arms, and by 1726, Maliseet, Passamaquoddy and Mi'kmaq chiefs, their people exhausted by the relentless violence, famine and misery, joined in. There followed an eighteen-year interval before the final conflict, but as usual, it was not without trouble.

Faced with a depressed fur market, Wabanakis increased their activities on the coast—in particular, going after seals and porpoises for their oil. This was in demand in the colonies and could be bartered for supplies formerly obtained in exchange for furs. At the same time, they faced increasing friction with Anglo fishermen, as on Matinicus Island in 1727. In February, a group of twelve Penobscots traveled there to hunt seals. Unfortunately, they found no seals and were marooned for several days by bad weather. To survive, they killed a cow and a hog that they found on the island, prompting expressions of outrage from the colonists.

Another problem was an English plan to harvest trees on the coast and islands for shipbuilding supplies. A new province between the Kennebec and Saint Croix Rivers would then be settled by hundreds of immigrants fleeing violence in Northern Ireland. As a consequence of all of this, the English hoped that "the Indians in a few years will be obliged to quitt that Country, for the settlements will drive all hunting far from them." In short, the English intended to violate their treaties (nothing new for them), threatening the Indians' natural resources and freedom of movement.

Fears of renewed warfare grew, and Penobscot and Passamaquoddy leaders Louis Neptune and Loron, along with Barenos de Saint-Castin, being warned of new hostilities, led a party of Wabanakis north to the St. Lawrence in Canada. The French, having declared war on Great Britain, resumed the usual conflicts in Wabanaki country. And once again, a bounty was placed on Indian scalps. In 1744, Governor William Shirley of Massachusetts promised payment of £100 for each Indian age twelve or older killed and £105 for each of like age captured. For women or children under age twelve killed, one would receive £50 or £55 plus plunder for captives. Another tactic, reported by a Catholic missionary, was distribution of infected clothing and blankets to Maliseets and Mi'kmaqs.

Not until 1749 was a treaty signed at Falmouth restoring peace. By then, Wabanaki economies were in ruins, but the treaty did restore "all their lands, liberties, and properties, not by them conveyed or sold to or possessed by any of the English subjects…as also the privilege of fishery, hunting, and fouling as formerly."

As before, peace remained elusive. For example, in 1751, a group of Indians on Matinicus Island, long valued as a place to hunt seals and birds and gather eggs, came up to the house of settler Ebenezer Hall. He had built his house on the island without a legal right to do so. Inside, Hall and his sons took their guns and shot their visitors down in cold blood. They then proceeded to cut and burn the Indians' canoe, saying, "Now we have killed the Devils, we will burn their damn'd canoo."

Although the murder was kept secret, Penobscots complained in 1755 to Massachusetts authorities about Hall, saying, "God has planted us here, God gave us this land: and we will keep it. God decreed all things; he decreed this land to us; therefore neither shall the French or English possess it, but we will."

Although Hall was ordered off the island, he did not comply, and in 1757, the Penobscots took matters into their own hands. Hall was killed and his family abducted. His wife was eventually repatriated, but the fate of his children is unknown. Perhaps they were killed, or perhaps they refused repatriation. We do know that a significant number of captives refused to return to colonial settlements when the opportunity came, preferring instead life in Indian communities. Some of these captives rose to become quite prominent, one being Joseph Louis Gill. He became known as the "White Chief" of St. Francis, the Mission village of Odanak in Québec where many Abenaki refugees from Maine and elsewhere in New England took up residence.

THE FINAL CONFLICT

The last conflict in which the French were involved, the French and Indian War, broke out in the same year as the Penobscot complaint about Ebenezer Hall. Much as they hated the English, who, in the words of anthropologists Prins and McBride, "had destroyed their villages, killed their game, dammed their rivers, cut their woods, murdered their relatives and ruined their lives," the Penobscots tried to stay out of the conflict. Being "on the front line," so to speak, they were more vulnerable to raiders and bounty hunters than other Wabanakis, who "took up the hatchet" with the French. The Penobscot claim of neutrality, however, was of no avail in the face of the colonial attitude that "if you are not with us, you're against us." Thus, in 1755, they were declared "enemies, rebels and traitors to his Majesty," and a

The proclamation of 1755 set a bounty on Penobscot Indian scalps. *Courtesy Abbe Museum.*

price was set on their heads. In 1756, the bounty was increased to £300 for a scalp and £320 for a captive. Again quoting Prins and McBride, "To be seen by the enemy was to be marked for death." If this wasn't bad enough, another epidemic of smallpox struck Wabanaki communities.

By 1759, the British had taken and fortified the Saint John River, leaving the Penobscot as the only outlet to the sea. Complaining that "the Penobscot Country…[was] a Den for Savages and a lurking place for some Renegadoe French [with] Indianized Frenchman intermixed with them," Governor Pownall of Massachusetts determined to remedy the situation. To do so, he built Fort Pownall at the mouth of the river, closing "the last and only door the enimy had left to the Atlantic." If the Indians contested his control, he vowed to "sweep it [the river] from one end to the other, and hunt ye all out."

In the same year, Quebec fell to the British, with Montreal following soon thereafter. With this, the French were swept from their holdings on mainland North America, leaving their Indian friends exposed and vulnerable, even though still in place. For the next 250 years, the Wabanakis were essentially on their own.

Chapter 4

Survival and Renewal in an Alien World

With the fall of Montréal in 1760, formalized by the Treaty of Paris in 1763, the last of the French and Indian wars came to an end, and a rush of English settlers began to arrive in the region east of the St. George River. Yet it is clear that significant numbers of Indians remained along the coast. In 1763, a Royal Proclamation decreed that English colonists were not allowed to settle east of the Penobscot River. However, a rather large exception was made to grant Governor Francis Bernard (who succeeded Pownall) Mount Desert Island. Otherwise, Indians were not to be disturbed Down East. But disturbed they were, by early settlers using a variety of devious tactics to occupy Indian lands. A case in point is early settlement of Mount Desert Island by Abraham Somes and Eben Sutton. In 1761, Somes prepared a place to squat and, a year later, brought his wife and children to live there. He later claimed that, on a fishing trip in 1755, he and Sutton had stopped off in Southwest Harbor, where they met "the island's governor." There followed negotiations to "buy" Greening's Island, the price being one gallon of rum. For his part, Sutton purchased the island that now bears his name for two quarts of rum. The completed transaction was recorded on a piece of birch bark, signed by the "Indian governor." Such "birch-bark deeds" obtained from any Indian who could be persuaded to sign, through drink or other devious methods, were common in seventeenth-century New England. In the case of Somes, it was conveniently lost in later years. In fact, his whole story was made up, but he was successful in establishing his right to settle.

All along the coast, similar strategies were used by English-speaking settlers to justify their takeover of Indian lands. When the Passamaquoddy chief Abowadwonit complained about occupancy of his people's ancestral land, Governor Bernard denied having authorized settlement on lands except those not inhabited for many years. In reality, such lands were not uninhabited but rather used on a seasonal basis. Their emptiness was an illusion; when the Indians were in one of their other seasonal camps, it only appeared that some lands stood empty.

Despite such problems, and a tendency to regroup in traditional villages, as that at Indian Island (Panawamské), Indian Township (Motohkomikuk) and Pleasant Point (Sipayik), the coast was not abandoned. For example, in 1767, John Billings built a log cabin in what is now the town of Brooksville, not far from the head of Walker's Pond, near an Indian village. He is said to have lived at peace with the Indians for several years, and his children played with their children. Surely, the village referred to is the one that had earlier served as Madockawando's headquarters, still in existence.

PENOBSCOTS, PASSAMAQUODDIES, MALISEETS
AND THE AMERICAN REVOLUTION

The head chief of the Penobscots at the time was Joseph Orono, who died in 1801. Though he lived upriver, he nonetheless spent considerable time in his family's ancestral homeland on the coast. According to his son-in-law, he was related to "Old Castine," evidently the son of one of the Baron's daughters and great-grandson of the Etchemin chief Madockawando. A boy named Joseph who was with Saint-Castin's daughter Claire when she was captured in 1704 by the British may have been this future chief. He was reputed to have lived for over one hundred years.

Orono was a tall, thin man with a pale complexion, blue eyes and reddish hair. He was devoted to the French and spoke their language as well as he did Penobscot. His nickname was K'tolaqu, meaning "frigate," because he talked so much about French warships that he had visited in 1780 when in Newport, Rhode Island, on a mission to request a priest from the French consul there. His animal emblem was the beaver.

When on the coast, Orono often stayed in the home of Seth Webb, who settled on Deer Isle in 1765. Together, the two would go hunting along the Union River and its tributaries. This friendship between Webb and Orono is of interest because Webb had been captured by Indians at his original home

Survival and Renewal in an Alien World

We have no image of Joseph Orono from his lifetime; this imagined image is from a fountain in Philadelphia's Fairmount Park West, dating from 1876, to honor Catholic veterans of the Revolutionary War. Photo by Wallace Haviland. *Collection of the author.*

in Windham, Maine, and then ransomed in 1752. Perhaps that experience resulted in a better understanding of the native people than was prevalent among the New England colonists.

With an eye to the future, Orono led a Penobscot delegation to meet the Provincial Congress of Massachusetts at Watertown mere days after the Battle of Bunker Hill. Upon his departure to offer the services of the Penobscots to the rebel cause, he addressed his people as follows:

> *Our white brothers tell us they came to the Indians country to enjoy liberty and life. A great sagamore (King George) is coming to bind them in chains, to kill them. We must fight him. We will stand on the same ground with them, for should he bind them in bonds, next he will treat us as bears. Indian liberties and land, his proud spirit will tear away from them. Help his ill-treated sons...Look down the stream of time. Look up to the Great Spirit. Be kind, be valiant, be free, then are Indians the sons of glory.*

At Watertown, the Penobscots agreed to side with the rebels in return for rights to six miles of land on each side of the river above the head of tide. True to their promise, the Penobscots fought at Castine in 1779 and, after the American defeat there, met with the authorities at Treat's Truck House near Bangor and, in defiance of Mohawk threats, pledged to stand with the colonists. Orono himself served the cause by carrying messages for the Americans to Machias, the Saint John River and Halifax. But true to form, Massachusetts reneged on its part of the bargain and, in 1796, forced Orono into signing a treaty to quit most of the land promised them on the river. This was subsequently divided into nine townships.

After the Revolution, Orono and his followers were frequently spotted on islands east of Deer Isle's Sunshine District, and one island off Swan's is even named for him. Following a split among the Penobscots shortly after 1783, he and a group of Catholic followers went with a Recollet missionary and established a headquarters on White Island, off Sunshine, with several wigwams and a chapel. At a meeting there in 1786, with Massachusetts commissioner Benjamin Lincoln, he complained bitterly about attempts by white settlers to evict him and his companions. It seems that, a year earlier, a settler who claimed ownership had proceeded to cut wood on the island and to burn the Indians' dwellings and chapel.

Not just the Penobscots, but the Passamaquoddies and Maliseets, too, were caught up in the Revolution. By 1777, Machias had become the easternmost stronghold of the fledgling United States or, in British eyes "a nest of pirates and rebels." Here, Colonel John Allen led a combined force of Indians and non-Indians. In an attempt to divide the Wabanakis, the British built Fort Howe at the mouth of the Saint John River and allowed a French Acadian priest to return to the valley. His job was to persuade Maliseets to come in on the British side. Some did, but others traveled to Machias, joining Passamaquoddy allies there. Under Colonel Allen's command, they were authorized to capture enemy vessels. In August 1777, they repelled an attack by five British naval vessels. Later, an armed schooner, seized by Passamaquoddy captain Sopiel Socktoma and fifty of his men, was brought into Machias.

Had it not been for the contributions of the three Wabanaki Nations—Maliseets, Passamaquoddies and Penobscots—all of Maine east of the Penobscot River today would probably be part of Canada. Without the Indians, the colonial forces were not up to the task of defending the territory. As for the British, they were fearful of declaring all-out war on the Indians loyal to the rebels, for fear that those Wabanakis who remained loyal to the Crown, or even just neutral, would take up arms in support of their kin. They could ill afford an Indian war in those colonies that remained loyal to Britain.

Like the Penobscots after the Revolution, the Passamaquoddies and Maliseets were betrayed not just by the United States but also by Britain. In the treaty ending the war, no consideration was given to the future of the Wabanaki Nations. Thus, the international boundary between Canada and the United States sliced right through Wabanaki territory, splitting Passamaquoddies and Maliseets on one side from their friends and relatives on the other. And on the Canadian side, Maliseets found themselves swamped by an influx of thousands of Tory refugees from the new United States. Eventually, they were left with six reserves along the Saint John River. At Qonasqamkuk (now Saint Andrews), an important Passamaquoddy gathering place, British Loyalists (many from Pentagöet) evicted the Indians, relocating them to an island in the bay. A subsequent displacement moved them to Sipayik (Pleasant Point) in Maine. To this day, the Canadian government has denied recognition of the Passamaquoddies on their side of the border.

COASTAL LIFE AFTER THE REVOLUTION

After the war, the Indians continued to experience hard times. Continued land clearing for farms and timber destroyed ever more habitat for game, adversely affecting hunting. Increased erosion from land clearing silted up streams and, in combination with dam building, had a similar effect on fishing. To compensate, Indians came to rely more and more on work as river drivers for the logging industry or, as the nineteenth century wore on, guides for out-of-state sport hunters. On the coast, porpoise hunting became a major activity. In this, the Passamaquoddies were particularly active, but Penobscots also participated.

As it happened, there was a burgeoning market for porpoise oil, and a single porpoise would yield an average of six to seven gallons. As fuel for many newly built or soon-to-be built lighthouses, porpoise oil was unsurpassed: it gave off good light, was unaffected by cold temperatures and was not smelly or sticky. The oil was also used for greasing both machinery and wool. An added bonus was a fatty mass at the root of the animal's jaw that yielded about a half pint of high-grade lubricant for watches.

As practiced around 1800, the Indians went out in twenty-foot birch-bark canoes, using guns to shoot the porpoises. (Before guns, bows and arrows were used for the shooting.) Nicholas Smith, a longtime student of Indian ways, describes what happened next:

> After the porpoise was shot, a canoe was paddled up to it. The Bowman killed it with a spear before grabbing it by sticking two fingers of his right hand into the blowhole and holding the pectoral fin with the left hand, hauling it up at least half its length before dragging it aboard, a tricky job when the catch was a large 300 pounder and a good sea was running. Boys were taken out when they were 10 or 12.

Manly Hardy, of Brewer, who knew the Indians better than most whites and who hunted porpoises with them, wrote the following in 1908:

This page: These three engravings show Passamaquoddy porpoise hunters off Grand Manan Island, about 1880. To shoot and then spear the animal, the bowman had to stand up in the canoe. This required great skill, especially if any sort of sea was running. *G.D. Good: The fisheries and fishing industries of the United States, Section 5, Plate 212. Washington: Government Printing Office, and* Scribner's Magazine, *October 6, 1880.*

Survival and Renewal in an Alien World

When the Indians in one canoe killed a porpoise, they "flashed" another canoe. The flashing was done by holding a wet paddle up and letting the sun strike it so as to throw a flash of sunlight that could be seen a mile, the aboriginal heliograph. The canoe flashed immediately gave up hunting and paddled to the canoe which had killed the porpoise, which was thrown into the second canoe to be taken care of.

One staging area for porpoise hunting, as well as fishing and clamming, in Blue Hill and Penobscot Bays was Black Island, west of Naskeag. It has since been renamed Conary Island for its first non-Indian occupant, who is said to have murdered an Indian then living there. Although supposedly reserved for the Penobscots by a treaty signed in 1796, interference in their traditional use of the island reached the point where a formal protest was made to state authorities in 1831 by Lieutenant Governor (second chief) John Neptune and Joseph SocBasin, asking that "all white people may be told to go away" so they might "use them [the islands] as their fathers have always done."

The Neptune family was a leading one among both Passamaquoddies and Penobscots. Among the latter, they were known as a "saltwater family," to distinguish them from "upriver families." These last were descendants of Abenaki refugees from the old Mawooshen Confederacy who became

John Neptune, lieutenant governor of the Penobscots, from a portrait painted circa 1840 by Jeremiah Pierson Hardy. The Neptunes are a prominent Etchemin family, whose ancestry includes Madockawando. *Courtesy Tarratine Club, Bangor.*

the majority among the Penobscot, whereas the saltwater families were descendants of the indigenous Etchemins. The Neptunes, in fact, were direct descendants of the old Grandchief Madockawando, although not through métis intermediaries, as was Orono. John Neptune was known in his day as an especially strong shaman, and he rose to become second chief (lieutenant governor) under John Attean. After allegedly seducing the latter's wife, leading to a rift between what were called the "New" and "Old" Parties, he went into exile, later gathering his family and relocating to Brewer. Although Neptune and Attean later reconciled, the split between parties continued. The state then stepped in and, with the agreement of the Penobscots, changed the term in office of chief from lifetime tenure to two years, with biannual elections.

Neptunes were especially prominent among the Passamaquoddies, where the position of head chief was held by members of this family for over two hundred years. One of them, Jean Baptiste, a grandson of Madockawando, served with several other Neptunes under Colonel Allen at Machias in the Revolution. Jean Baptiste died there in 1778, at age sixty, and was succeeded as chief by his son, the third Neptune to hold that office. According to Fannie Hardy Eckstorm, whose knowledge of these matters is unsurpassed, the Neptunes removed eastward in 1726 after one of them signed the treaty ending the fourth Wabanaki War. Thereafter, Neptunes are found among the Passamaquoddies and Maliseets, where Etchemins remained in the majority, and even Mi'kmaqs. Eventually, some returned to the Penobscots. All of this illustrates the linkages through kinship between all of the Wabanaki Nations. Kinship, rather than territoriality was, and remains, the chief organizing principle among them. And today, there isn't a Penobscot without Passamaquoddy kin, and vice versa.

In the nineteenth century, as the years passed, Wabanakis found themselves increasingly restricted by the growing population and actions of non-Indians. Reduced to living on the margins of an alien society not of their own making, they turned increasingly to new ways of making a living. Besides porpoise hunting, log driving and guiding out-of-state hunters and others (probably the most famous being Henry David Thoreau in 1846, 1855 and 1857), they began making craft items of wood, including tubs, boxes, toys, broomsticks, axe handles and baskets. These they sold door-to-door from camps near white settlements. Though produced to appeal to non-Indian customers, these crafts, like porpoise hunting and guiding outsiders in the woods, were based on old established indigenous traditions and skills.

Survival and Renewal in an Alien World

Although the initial market for craft items was local, it began to expand in the 1840s as the "rusticator era" began. This arose as a reaction to living in newly industrializing cities that, in the summer, were hot, dirty and unhealthy. Those urban dwellers who could afford it headed for cooler climates where they could experience clean, healthy country living. Typically, men would ship wives and children off for the summer, visiting them for brief periods as time and transportation permitted. One such destination was Mount Desert Island, which grew to become a major summer resort as wealthy industrialists, artists and other prominent individuals came, bought property and built often lavish summer "cottages."

Vast new markets for Indian craft items, especially ash splint and sweet grass baskets tailored to Victorian tastes, were opened up by this influx of outsiders. In the 1840s, Penobscot and Passamaquoddy families began selling their wares to the rusticators. By the 1860s, Mount Desert Island was a major destination to which these Wabanakis came, some by canoe, others traveling by train and steamboat. Bar Harbor became the center

Shore-side view of the Indian encampment at the foot of Bar/ Bridge Street, Bar Harbor, 1881. *Photo by Kilburn Brothers. Courtesy of Dee Lustusky and the Abbe Museum.*

of activities, with major encampments of Indians. Besides selling craft items ranging from snowshoes and canoes to baskets and toys, they also provided hunting and canoeing services. These encampments lasted into the 1920s, the peak population around 1885 being about 250 mostly Penobscots and Passamaquoddies.

At the time all this was happening, two stereotypes of Indians competed for acceptance by whites. One was the "dirty, drunken savage, destined to disappear," and in the nineteenth century, almost every town had a story (usually untrue) of the last Indian to live there. The other was the romantic idea of the Indian leading an idyllic existence as part of an unspoiled "natural world." It was this latter stereotype that prevailed among the rusticators and others in the Northeast, even as the Indian Wars were taking place out West. In the Northeast, however, Indians had long since ceased to be a threat, and the "noble savage" idea fit right in with the glorification of nature then popular in art and literature. Still, among hardscrabble farmers living in the backcountry, one could find lingering resentment of Indians, who were treated by the state as ignorant, incompetent and incapable of managing their own affairs.

Although Bar Harbor was the summer destination of the greatest number of Wabanakis, it was not the only one. Small families of Penobscots and Passamaquoddies traveled to other parts of the state and even farther afield in the Northeast. Illustrative is Frank Loring, more widely known by his stage name of "Chief Big Thunder." Born in 1827 to a Penobscot mother and a mixed Portuguese/Wampanoag father, he was the youngest of eight children, and his mother died when he was eight. To survive, he and his sisters took up basketry, and he traveled widely in the Northeast selling baskets. In the 1840s, he spent eight months or so working for P.T. Barnum and then the next five decades producing, directing and acting in Indian entertainments—then quite popular—all over New England. Besides his career as a showman, he was also a skilled hunter, trapper, canoeist, orator and storyteller. And like his mother, he was well versed in traditional healing methods.

Frank Loring was big physically—six-foot-four and 225 pounds—as well as in personality. He spent much of his time in the summers on Mount Desert Island, where he was a well-known fixture, but he still led the kind of mobile lifestyle traditionally favored by his people. He would periodically leave his establishment at Bar Harbor and is remembered as camping in the 1880s on Eagle Island (in the middle of Penobscot Bay) and the seaward end of Isle au Haut with his companion, Passamaquoddy chief Joe Dana. In both places, the two of them hunted seals, porpoises and birds.

Frank Loring, widely known as "Chief Big Thunder," from a postcard. *Courtesy Abbe Museum.*

At age seventy-two, Big Thunder is said to have embarked on a journey in a traditional bark canoe, dressed in deerskin clothing and with a birch wigwam. His destination was Washington, D.C., and his purpose was to plead with President McKinley to save his people. On the way, he ate nothing but gulls' eggs and fish, making fire the old-fashioned way, without matches. But his strength gave out, and he had to turn back, having gotten nearly halfway down the New England coast. Still, he remained active, and two years after this trip, he was elected lieutenant governor of the Penobscots, their second-highest office. Earlier, he had served as wampum keeper and in various other positions. Late in life, he served as one of anthropologist Frank Speck's informants for his classic ethnography, *Penobscot Man.* He was still working a few months before his death on a new Indian play to be performed in Lewiston.

In his storytelling and entertainment, Frank Loring was not averse to exaggeration and giving his audience what they expected to hear and see, playing on their stereotypes. Consequently, some outsiders were inclined to see him as a fraud. As anthropologist Gordon Day put it: "All who knew him agreed that he was unscrupulous, a liar, and a rascal." This misses the point, for in fact he was a cultural survivalist. As anthropologist Harald Prins points out: "He understood the importance of his 'Indian' identity, refused to walk the assimilation path, took a critical stance toward the dominant culture, was not above creatively fooling the affluent white folk visiting his humble abode and milking them for all they were worth."

Watching the traditional culture bleed from his community, he became Big Thunder, the trickster (like the great Gluskabe), engaged in a "subversive strategy of creative resistance in the form of theatrics."

Big Thunder was not alone. At the end of the century, other Indians traveled to Eagle Island to sell their craft items to summer boarders and to gather sweet grass. They would come from Castine Harbor, portaging across Cape Rosier, stopping on the way at Hog Island, where there were

This photo from the 1890s shows Wabanakis paddling seagoing canvas canoes on the Isle au Haut Thorofare. At the time, they camped at the west end of the thorofare, but they sold their baskets to rusticators in a summer colony at the east end. *Photo by John C. Turner. Courtesy Deer Isle-Stonington Historical Society.*

also summer boarders. Next to Eagle was Butter Island, developed as a summer resort and another market for baskets and such. From Eagle, they crossed the three miles of open water to Sunset Village in Deer Isle, where another summer colony had sprung up. Down the bay on Isle au Haut, Indians peddled their wares to a developing summer colony there.

In 1897, Joe Dana, head chief at Sipayik (Pleasant Point), camped with a group of Passamaquoddies on Saddleback Island, off Stonington (on Deer Isle). They came in four canoes and, while there, made rustic chairs and settees. These they took into Stonington for sale. They also hunted seagulls, with guns and ammunition supplied by a New York millinery dealer. At the time, the dealer would pay forty cents for each adult gull and twenty cents for immature ones, gull breasts and feathers being in high demand to decorate the hats of fashionable ladies in New York and other cities. This activity decimated gull populations, but the Passamaquoddies were glad for the income. By this time, the game they traditionally hunted was scarce, owing to habitat destruction and the influx of out-of-state hunters. To make matters worse, in the 1880s the state started enforcing hunting and fishing regulations on Indians, despite treaties recognizing their traditional rights. Unable to get sufficient food for their families, infant mortality skyrocketed

The settee shown in this picture is one of the pieces of rustic furniture made by Passamaquoddies camped on Saddleback Island back in 1898 or '99 and sold in Stonington. *Courtesy of Neva Beck.*

on the Passamaquoddy reservations. Small wonder that they would take advantage of the opportunity to earn a little money.

In the 1920s, the Indian campsite at Bar Harbor fell into disuse, but this did not mean that Wabanakis had abandoned the area. Instead, they lived scattered about at different locations on Mount Desert Island. Passamaquoddy John Snow, for example, had established a small basket shop in Northeast Harbor in 1907, where he lived with his family until his death twenty-seven years later. Frequently, he was visited by other Indians, who stayed at his house. Other Wabanakis were to be found at several other places around the island; besides gathering sweet grass and selling baskets, many took up work as day laborers or in the numerous canneries then in operation. Big Thunder's granddaughter was one of the latter, working for seventy-five years, beginning in 1907, in fish factories in Bass Harbor and Southwest Harbor.

Wabanakis continued their activities elsewhere, as well. On Deer Isle, Lawrence Mitchell and his family came every summer from Indian Island to Sunset, from at least 1927 into the 1950s. From a canvas tent by the road known as the "Indian camp" and, in later years, by going door-to-door, they sold the usual assortment of baskets and other items. They were respected by members of the community who regularly addressed them as "Mr." and "Mrs.," and their activities were noted along with those of other locals and rusticators in the Deer Isle newspaper, the *Messenger*.

That this family chose Sunset as their summer home was no accident. A first cousin of Lawrence's grandfather, Charlie "Daylight" Mitchell, is known to have frequented Sunset, following the old route from Eagle Island between 1907 and 1918. (The old nickname "Daylight" stems from the family's reputation as early risers.) In fact, the Mitchell family had a connection with the Deer Isle region going back hundreds of years. Lawrence's mother, Sarah Susep, was also from a family long associated with the coast. The families' traditional animal names were Lobster (Mitchell) and Crab (Susep), and their headquarters were at the mouth of the Bagaduce and Stockton, respectively. The Mitchells (surely) and the Suseps (possibly) must have, many generations back, been part of Madockawando's regional band and therefore of Etchemin descent. The Mitchells were reputed to be expert seafarers and saltwater canoeists and were one of the last Penobscot families to subsist predominantly on resources from the sea.

Lawrence Mitchell did not rely solely on the sale of baskets and craft items. He also had a full-time job as a printer and later compositor with the *Bangor Daily News*. During the week, he would leave his family in Sunset, returning on weekends. Thus, his job did not prevent him from maintaining a connection with the family's ancient home territory.

The Mitchells were not the only Wabanakis active around Penobscot Bay in the twentieth century. Others canoed to the north end of Little Deer Isle from Brooksville at least twice a summer through the 1920s. Their destination was another summer colony, where there was a market for baskets and beaded moccasins. Another was Joseph Lauren, identified as an "Old Town Indian," who camped at several spots around Deer Isle and Little Deer. A fiddle player, he would sometimes play for dances. Also on Deer Isle was Rose Dunbar, who was part Penobscot and was the matriarch of an extended family living in tarpaper shacks in an enclave of their own on a tidal creek. Neither she nor Joseph Lauren (Lauren is a variant of the name Loring, the family name also of "Big Thunder") appear on the official roster of the Penobscot Nation, probably because both were married to non-Indians, something that was not legal in Maine. Old diaries and family traditions mention other Indians, but these mentions are so brief that next to nothing is known of them. Surely, Mount Desert Island and Deer Isle are not alone as places where Indians were present into recent times. Intensive research of the sort undertaken at these two places would surely reveal similar situations elsewhere along the coast. Though outnumbered by the descendants of Europeans, Wabanakis remained there in small but strong family bands.

Other Wabanakis traveled farther afield; Louis Sockalexis, for example, left Indian Island to play professional baseball for Cleveland from 1897 to 1899 (and it was for him that the team came to be called the Indians) or Molly Nelson, whose stage name was "Spotted Elk," who gained fame as a dancer in the United States and Paris and the female lead in the 1930s film *Silent Enemy*. But always, these individuals had Indian Island to return to, where they could renew their ties to their people and their sense of who they were.

THE MODERN RESURGENCE

Another entertainer who left Indian Island was Lucy Nicolar, whose stage name was "Princess Watahwaso," daughter of Penobscot Joseph Nicolar, author of the classic *Life and Traditions of the Red Man*. Joseph's father, Tomar Nicola, was a descendant of a refugee from the 1724 Norridgewock massacre, while his mother was the daughter of Mary Malt Neptune, whose father was John Neptune. Thus, Joseph Nicolar was of both Etchemin and Abenaki ancestry and, through the Neptunes, a descendant of Madockawando.

The Nicolar family traveled, like so many others each summer, to the coast—in their case, Kennebunkport. Here, they sold the usual baskets, while Lucy and her sister Florence, dressed in Indian outfits, sang and danced for potential customers. In 1894, when their father died, the two, with their mother, began taking part in sportsmen's exhibitions in Boston, New York and Baltimore. Eventually, Lucy went on to be a professional entertainer, meeting and later marrying Bruce Poolaw, a Kiowa. Florence married fellow Penobscot Leo Shay, and the two moved to Connecticut to take advantage of employment opportunities there. When the Depression hit, however, and jobs dried up, the Shays returned to Indian Island.

An accomplished basket maker, Florence and her husband, Leo, set up a tent each summer at Lincolnville Beach on Penobscot Bay, where they sold baskets. Though reserved by nature, Florence was an indefatigable activist, working for decades to secure better education for Penobscot children, Indian voting rights and a bridge from Indian Island to the mainland.

Collaborating with Florence in her advocacy was her sister Lucy, whose more extroverted style complemented Florence's reserve. With the Depression, she and Bruce Poolaw also returned to Indian Island. There, the two of them ran an Indian novelty shop out of a wooden tipi called Chief Poolaw's Teepee where the bridge meets the island. Florence's son Charles has refurbished his aunt's tipi, as well as the Poolaw house, where he now lives. A highly decorated combat veteran of World War II and the Normandy landings, Charles lived for many years in Austria with the wife he met there, working for the International Atomic Energy Agency and the United Nations high commissioner of refugees.

In 2002, Charles returned to Indian Island. Five years later, the French consul general from Boston traveled to Indian Island, Maine, and escorted Charles to Washington to the residence of the French ambassador, where President Sarcozy awarded him the Légion d'Honneur, France's highest decoration. This is bestowed on individuals who have made an extraordinary contribution to the French nation. It's an extremely rare honor, especially for a foreigner. A modest man, Charles seeks no recognition for himself but rather to remind people of the bravery and sacrifice of other Indian veterans whose service to the United States is at risk of being lost to history. Despite having lived in Austria for thirty-nine years, Charles is terribly proud of his Penobscot heritage and has converted the big wooden tipi from which his aunt and her husband, Bruce Poolaw, once sold Indian craft items into a family museum.

When Charles Shay returned from World War II, conditions on the reservation were not good. At the time, negative stereotypes were quite common, as illustrated when, in 1945, the Shays and Poolaws went together to Old Town to vote in a local election. With Charles, a highly decorated combat veteran and former POW, in his dress uniform, studded with medals, at the head of the line, they were told: "Idiots don't have any right to vote in this state." Not until 1953 could Maine's Indians vote in national elections; the right to vote in local and state elections did not come until 1967.

Yet through the efforts of individuals like Florence and Lucy, things began to change, not just for the Penobscots but

Penobscot elder Charles Norman Shay, wearing his military decorations. *Photograph by Anita de Laguna Haviland.*

for the Passamaquoddies, Maliseets and Mi'kmaqs as well. A renaissance began to take place, culminating in the Maine Indian Land Claims Settlement, signed into law by President Carter in 1980.

It started on the Passamaquoddy reservation at Indian Township in 1957. At the time, conditions there were particularly bad; almost 75 percent of the people were unemployed, the majority was on welfare, many were suffering from alcoholism and the residents were regarded with scorn by non-Indians. It was at this point that John Stevens, the Passamaquoddy governor, was shown a treaty by his great-aunt Louise Sockabasin that she had tucked away in a shoebox. Dating from 1794, the treaty was with Massachusetts and recognized Indian title to twenty-three thousand acres, fifteen islands in the St. Croix River, two islands in Big Lake and ten acres (later expanded to one hundred) at Pleasant Point. By 1957, none of the islands remained in Passamaquoddy ownership, and their land in Indian Township had been reduced to seventeen thousand acres. Over the years, the state had sold off much of their land, as well as rights to timber and grass. To make matters worse, the funds held in trust from these sales had been badly mismanaged.

After being shown this treaty, Stevens tried to rally his people around the issue of encroachment on Passamaquoddy land, but he had little success in the face of widespread despondency. Then, in 1964, this all changed when John's brother, George, was disturbed by a non-Indian owner of some tourist cabins who was clearing land to expand his operation. He had acquired this land in a poker game with another white man, who claimed that the state had validated his title to it. With this latest encroachment on their land, the Passamaquoddies said, "Enough!" Six of them, led by the two Stevens brothers, went to Augusta to request that the state resolve the issue, as required by law. After being kept waiting for five hours, the request was basically dismissed by the governor and the attorney general. The Passamaquoddies protested by holding a sit-in on a road being built into the property, resulting in the arrest of five of the female protesters. With this, the Indians decided to go to court seeking restoration of the six thousand acres of land lost since the 1794 treaty was signed.

The case dragged on for several years until, in 1969, a newly graduated lawyer named Thomas Tureen, took on the case. Having witnessed how the government in South Dakota treated Indians, he abandoned the study of literature and poetry and, in 1967, clerked for the Passamaquoddies' lawyer. Putting together a team of independent financial backers and legal experts, the conclusion was reached in 1972 that the only way to proceed was for the federal government, in fulfillment of its constitutional responsibilities to Indians, to sue the state. With the support of a new governor and the state's entire congressional delegation, they submitted a formal petition to the commissioner of Indian affairs, a request the commissioner supported (ironic, since he was a Mohawk, a nation that three hundred years earlier was a sworn enemy of the Wabanakis).

In spite of the commissioner's support, not to mention that of Maine's elected officials, officials in Washington dragged their heels, waiting for a statute of limitation to expire in July 1972. So in June, the legal team filed suit against the secretary of the interior requesting a court order that he file a suit against the state. After much legal maneuvering, a judge ordered the Department of Justice to proceed with the case against the State of Maine. Two weeks before the statute of limitations was to run out, the government agreed to add the Penobscots to the case.

The key to the whole case was the Federal Trade and Non-intercourse Act passed by Congress in 1790. It clearly specifies that no transfer of Indian land, to states or anyone else, can take place without the express approval of Congress. Not only had it not approved sales of Passamaquoddy land, but neither had it done so for the Penobscot. In their case, in treaties with Massachusetts, they gave up nearly 200,000 acres in 1796 and, in 1818, ceded all other lands except the islands in the river above Old Town and four townships of six square miles. In 1833, they lost the four townships to the State of Maine in a transaction involving forged signatures. All of these were in violation of the 1790 act. The upshot was that the state was liable for 12.5 million acres, nearly a third of the state.

At first, a new governor and attorney general in Augusta refused to take the land claims seriously, but when municipalities found that they could not issue bonds in the disputed area and that it might be impossible to transfer real estate or obtain mortgages, attitudes changed. Meanwhile, the commissioner of Indian affairs determined that the Passamaquoddies and Penobscots were entitled to $5 million a year in benefits for housing, education, healthcare and other social services.

Over the next four years, there was considerable legal and political maneuvering, including demagoguery on the part of the governor and attempts by the state's congressional delegation to extinguish the claims. Early in the Carter administration, the president himself got involved, appointing a special representative to evaluate the claims. Because the lawsuits would have a devastating impact on the state, the president's representative advised not going to trial. Instead, he recommended a negotiated settlement, something that the Indians had been trying to do since 1976. Over the next several months, a three-man task force appointed by the White House and an eleven-man Passamaquoddy-Penobscot negotiating committee got down to serious bargaining. The sessions were boycotted by the state, which loudly denounced a proposed agreement. With elections coming up, anti-Indian sentiment among voters was whipped up by politicians.

Ultimately, the state came to the table, and a settlement was worked out, signed by President Carter on October 10, 1980. By its provisions, the Indians would get $81.5 million, to be split between a trust fund and the purchase of land to add to the 100,000 acres given them outright. In return, they would extinguish their claim against all the defendants in the case. In addition, they would be eligible for federal programs and services available to Indians. Along with this went sovereignty, though limited, as we shall see. To deal with conflicts over sovereignty issues, a State-Tribal Commission was established. This now consists of thirteen members, two each from the Holton Band of Maliseets, Passamaquoddies and Penobscots and six from the state, with the thirteenth selected by the other twelve. Finally, the Houlton band of Maliseets, an impoverished and landless group that survived in Aroostook County, was added to the settlement. They have since been able to acquire some 800 acres for themselves. Somehow, a group of Mi'kmaqs resident in the county was overlooked but, in 1991, gained federal recognition, making them eligible for federal financial assistance and services.

Since the days of the dispute over land claims, things have improved for the four Wabanaki Nations in Maine. This is not to say that things are as good as they could be, for they are not. There remains too much poverty among them. Still, they have more control over their own destinies, no longer being wards of the state. There is, however a problem here. The sovereignty granted them makes them equivalent to a municipality, subject to state taxes and laws. This is not equivalent to the sovereignty enjoyed by the federally recognized tribes west of the original thirteen states, where the reservations are, in effect, nations within the nation. This is a sore point and a source of constant friction. Moreover, there are lingering bits of prejudice, as can be seen in the statewide referendums over casino gambling. Routinely, proposals from both Penobscots and Passamaquoddies are voted down, whereas those for white-run operations have been successful. If Maine's Wabanakis had the same degree of sovereignty as the western tribes (which the Mi'kmaq, with their separate act of recognition may have), then the state, by federal law, would be required to "negotiate in good faith" a deal for Indian gaming.

Another example of lingering prejudice may be seen at the top of Caterpillar Hill in the town of Sedgwick. Here, beside the highway, the state Department of Transportation maintains a scenic turnout from which motorists can enjoy one of the great panoramic views in the state of Maine. Before them is spread out the whole of Penobscot Bay. In 2004, three granite monuments were placed here, each with etched photos and text. One relates to the geological history of the area; the other two deal with the histories of the nearby towns. So we jump from pre-human times to recent times, without a single mention of the people who lived in between. Not only did Indians live here longer than anyone else, but also their living sites are particularly numerous here, and as we have seen, their history in the region is a rich one. Although the monuments are a mere mile from Madockawando's headquarters, it's as if his people never existed!

On the positive side, it is testimony to Wabanaki creativity that they have been able to survive through four centuries of turmoil and upheaval and still maintain their distinct cultural identity. From a low point around 1822, when only 277 Penobscots remained, they have rebounded, and in 2012,

Survival and Renewal in an Alien World

The monuments at the scenic turnout on Caterpillar Hill in Sedgwick, Maine. The one on the right is titled "The Story of the Rocks"; the other two are stories of nearby towns. Visible behind them is Walker's Pond, where Madockawando had his headquarters, and beyond that Penobscot Bay. None of the monuments mentions indigenous inhabitants. *Photo by the author.*

they now number almost 2,400. The Passamaquoddies have undergone a similar resurgence; in 1850, there were about 400 of them, but now there are over 3,300. Maliseets today number between 6,000 and 7,000, all but a few hundred of whom live on the Canadian side of the border. Between the three nations, they now number more than there were Etchemins living in all of Ketakamigwa when Champlain met with Bashaba in 1604.

This resurgence has come in spite of concerted efforts on the part of governments to do away with Indians through assimilation, if possible. The prevailing attitude well into the twentieth century was that they had to conform to European-American culture or be crushed. Playing a key role in this were boarding schools to which many Wabanaki children were sent, frequently being taken from their families by force. Many from Maine went to the Carlisle Indian school in Pennsylvania, which was established in 1879 on what had been a military base. Here, cavalry officers had trained to fight against Indians. In Canada, Maliseets were sent to a comparable institution at Shubenacadie, Nova Scotia, established in 1930. At both schools, the philosophy was: "We must kill the Indian to save the man."

At these schools, discipline was harsh. Upon their arrival at Carlisle, the children's clothes and belongings were stripped from them, their hair was cut and boys were dressed in military-style uniforms and girls in "proper"

115

dresses. In both schools, they were forbidden to speak their own language, even if they knew no English. If they were caught doing so, the mildest punishment was to have their mouths washed out with soap. Travel home was prevented and communication with their families discouraged. At every opportunity, they were made to understand that Indians were evil, heathen and savage. For the most part, their education was training for menial jobs; girls were taught to sew, iron and do laundry. For boys, it was vocational trades such as carpentry, blacksmithing, printing or tailoring. Academic pursuits were considered beyond them. Infractions of rules were met by lashings with leather belts, other physical abuse or even jail.

The results of this regime were disastrous. Many students sickened and died or, in several instances, committed suicide. Those who survived the ordeal often found they had lost so much of their culture that they no longer fit into their home communities. Many even lost the ability to communicate with loved ones. To make matters worse, neither were they accepted into white society.

The Carlisle school shut down in 1918, but Shubenacadie did not close its doors until 1960. Even then, however, the practice of uprooting children from their communities did not end. During the 1950s and '60s in Maine, the federal Indian Adoption Project removed a number of Wabanaki children for adoption in non-Indian families. After that, the State Department of Health and Human Services continued to remove children it considered "at risk," favoring their placement in non-Indian foster homes. Of course, such policies fly in the face of native traditions in which children are not the responsibility of their family alone but of the whole community. There are always people to look out for them. Yet it was not until 1999 that the state backed off the practice of placement in nonnative homes.

On May 24, 2011, Maine governor Paul LePage and the chiefs of the four Wabanaki Nations gathered on Indian Island to sign An Intent to Establish a Child Welfare Truth and Reconciliation Commission. (In 1998, the Canadian government apologized for past wrongs.) Shown here from left to right are Passamaquoddy chiefs Joseph Socabasin (Indian Township), Reuben Cleaves (Pleasant Point), Governor LePage and Penobscot chief Kirk Francis. *Courtesy* Bangor Daily News.

As the numbers of Etchemin descendants and other Wabanakis have increased, so have they become more visible, particularly in the late twentieth and early twenty-first centuries. In Maine's public schools, state law dating from 2001 requires that Wabanaki culture and history be included in the K–12 curriculum. Then, too, there are public events, such as the yearly basket-maker sales and demonstrations in December at the Hudson Museum in Orono. In Bar Harbor, there is an annual Native American Festival in the summer on the campus of the College of the Atlantic. A partner in these events is the Maine Indian Basketmakers Alliance, founded by the four Wabanaki Nations in 1993 to preserve the traditions of ash and sweet grass basketry. Another partner in the Bar Harbor festival is the Abbe Museum, which also presents frequent craft workshops throughout the year. Wabanakis serve on the museum's board, as well, and periodically mount exhibits. Indeed, between year-round and seasonal visits, the flow of native people onto Mount Desert Island surely rivals that of the late 1800s and probably pre-colonial times.

Despite their problematic relationship with the state, three of Maine's four Wabanaki Nations have representatives in the legislature. Although they cannot vote, they can introduce legislation and speak. This arrangement began with the Penobscots, before Maine became a state, in 1820. Before this, they were accustomed to sending their leading men to the General Court of Massachusetts and, after statehood, to the legislature in Augusta. In 1842, the Passamaquoddies joined the practice. A year later, the legislature restricted the two nations to one elected representative each, an arrangement that continued until 1941. At that point, the legislature removed the Indians' seating and speaking privileges, reducing them to observer status. Their seating and speaking privileges were later restored in 1975, and in 2011, it was voted to add a representative of the Houlton Band of Maliseets. And in the twenty-first century, the practice of an annual address by the chiefs to the legislature was instituted.

The experience of Wabanakis in Maine and New Brunswick since 1604 has in many ways been similar to those of indigenous peoples the world over: frequently, they find they must forfeit their indigenous identity and be pressed into a mold that allows them no opportunity or motivation to rise above the lowest rung of the social ladder. From an autonomous people with pride and a strong sense of their own identity, they are all too often transformed into a deprived underclass with neither pride nor a sense of identity. The Wabanakis chose another way. As have indigenous peoples in virtually all parts of the globe, they have decided that they have a right to their own identity and should be allowed to work out their own way of participating in the modern world. When a whole people give up and disappear just because their continued presence is inconvenient or annoying to some, all of humanity is in trouble. The Wabanakis have not only not given up and

Eagle-topped monument by Penobscot sculptor Tim Shay, with the inscription: "This Memorial is dedicated to all Native American Warriors, Especially Wabanaki Warriors: Penobscot, Passamaquoddy, Maliseet, Micmac." Starting with the Revolution, Wabanakis have fought for the United States in all of its subsequent wars. *Photo by Anita de Laguna Haviland.*

disappeared, but they also display renewed vitality. In the words of Jennifer Neptune, member of a family with Etchemin roots:

> *If our ancestors were to return today, they would not recognize our clothing, cars or housing, but they would recognize the artists and their ways. In our communities they would still hear the rhythmic sound of an ash log being pounded for baskets, smell the sweet grass and freshly split ash in the basketmaker's homes, watch with pride as carvers transformed birch roots into war clubs; they would go for a spin in a freshly made birchbark canoe, savor a steaming hot bowl of fiddleheads, moose stew, or hulled corn soup, and finish off the day sitting around the fire laughing at old stories while listening to our drummers sing our ancient songs.*

Bibliography

Brodeur, Paul. "Restitution." *New Yorker*, October 11, 1982.

Bruchac, Joseph. *The Wind Eagle and Other Abenaki Stories*. Greenfield Center, NY: Bowman Books, 1985.

Butler, Eva L., and Wendell S. Hadlock. *Uses of Birch Bark in the Northeast*. Bar Harbor, ME: Robert Abbe Museum, Bulletin VII, 1957.

Cook, David S. *Above the Gravel Bar*. Solon, ME: Polar Bear and Co., 2007.

Coon, Carleton S. *Adventures and Discoveries*. Englewood Cliffs, NJ: Prentice Hall, 1981.

Cox, Steven L. "Archaeological Investigations at the Scott's Midden Site, Deer Isle." *Maine Archaeological Society Bulletin* 49, no. 2 (2009): 5–15.

Day, Gordon M. "The Penobscot War Bow." *In Search of New England's Native Past*. Edited by Michael K. Foster and William Cowan, 148–59. Amherst: University of Massachusetts Press, 1998.

Deal, Michael. *Lecture Notes for Anthropology 3291: Prehistory of the Maritime Provinces*. Memorial University of Newfoundland, posted on website, 2001 and 2006.

Eckstorm, Fannie H. *Handicrafts of the Modern Indians of Maine*. Bar Harbor, ME: Abbe Museum, 2003.

———. "Indian Place Names of the Penobscot Valley and the Maine Coast." *Maine Studies* 55 (1941).

———. *Old John Neptune and Other Maine Shamans*. Orono: University of Maine, 1980.

Fischer, David Hackett. *Champlain's Dream*. New York: Simon and Schuster, 2008.

Francis, David A., and Robert M. Leavitt. *A Passamaquoddy-Maliseet Dictionary*. Orono, ME: University of Maine Press, 2008.

Gerber, Ray R, and Mark H. Hedden. *Song of the Drum: The Petroglyphs of Maine*. DVD. Brunswick, ME: Acadia Productions, 2004.

Haviland, William A. *At the Place of the Lobsters and Crabs: Indian People and Deer Isle, Maine, 1605–2005*. Solon, ME: Polar Bear and Co., 2009.

———. *Deer Isle's Original People*. Deer Isle, ME: self-published, 2003.

———. *The Present Status of the Archaeology of Maine*. Master's thesis. Philadelphia: University of Pennsylvania, 1958.

Haviland, William A., and Marjory W. Power. *The Original Vermonters* (revised and expanded edition). Hanover, NH: University Press of New England, 1994.

Malone, Patrick M. *The Skulking Way of War*. Baltimore, MD: Johns Hopkins University, 1993.

McBride, Bunny, and Harald E.L. Prins. *Indians in Eden, Wabanakis and Rusticators on Maine's Mount Desert Island, 1840s–1920s*. Camden, ME: Down East Books, 2009.

Neptune, Jennifer. "Wabanaki Traditional Arts: From Old Roots to New Life." In *North by Northeast*. Edited by Kathleen Mundell, 25–27. Gardiner, ME: Tilbury House, 2008.

Nicolar, Joseph. *The Life and Traditions of the Red Man*. Edited and annotated by Annette Kolodny. Durham, NC: Duke University Press, 2007.

Prins, Harald E.L. *The Mi'kmaq: Resistance, Accommodation, and Cultural Survival*. Fort Worth, TX: Harcourt Brace, 1996.

Prins, Harald E.L., and Bunny McBride. *Asticou's Island Domain: Wabanaki Peoples at Mount Desert Island 1500–2000*. Boston, MA: National Park Service, 2007.

Robinson, Brian S. "'Archaic Period' Traditions of New England and the Northeast." *SAA Archaeological Record*, November 2008.

Robinson, Brian S., Jennifer C. Ort, William Eldridge, Adrian L. Burke and Bertrand G. Pelletier. "Paleoindian Aggregation and Social Context at Bull Brook." *American Antiquity* 74, no. 3 (2009): 423–47.

Rolde, Neil. *Unsettled Past, Unsettled Future, The Story of Maine Indians*. Gardiner, ME: Tilbury House, 2004.

Sanger, David. "Birchbark Canoes, Dugouts, and Gouges: Is There any Logical Relationship?" *Maine Archaeological Society Bulletin* 49, no. 2 (2009): 17–34.

———. "Insights into Native American Life at Fernald Point." In *An Island in Time, Three Thousand Years of Cultural Exchange on Mount Desert Island*, 5–20. Bar Harbor, ME: Abbe Museum, 1994.

———. "Late Archaic Period Swordfish Hunting: An Ethnoarchaeological Approach." *Maine Archaeological Society Bulletin* 49, no. 1 (2009): 7–22.

Smith, Nicholas N. "The Wabanaki as Mariners." In *Papers of the 24th Algonquian Conference*. Edited by William Cowan, 364–80. Ottawa: Carleton University, 1993.

Speck, Frank G. *Penobscot Man*. Orono: University of Maine Press, 1997.

———. "Penobscot Shamanism." *Memoirs of the American Anthropological Association* 6 (1920): 239–88.

———. "Penobscot Tales and Religious Beliefs." *Journal of American Folklore* 48 (1935): 187.

Spiess, Arthur, Kristin Sobolik, Diana Crader, John Mosher and Deborah Wilson. "Cod, Clams and Deer: The Food Remains from Indiantown Island." *Archaeology of Eastern North America* 34 (2006): 141–87.

University of Maine at Farmington Archaeology Research Center and the Passamaquoddy Tribe. *N'tolonapemk, An Ancient Village on Meddybemps Lake, Maine*. Pamphlet in possession of the author.

Whitehead, Ruth H. "The Traditional Material Culture of the Native Peoples of Maine." In *Twelve Thousand Years, American Indians in Maine*, by Bruce J. Bourque, 249–309. Lincoln: University of Nebraska Press, 2001.

The above references were consulted specifically for this book, but I have been influenced as well by forty-eight additional sources listed in the bibliography for my book *At the Place of the Lobsters and Crabs* and another forty-four in that for my 1958 master's thesis. Both works appear in the listing above.

Index

About the Author

D r. William A. Haviland is professor emeritus at the University of Vermont, where he founded the Department of Anthropology and taught for thirty-five years. He holds a PhD in anthropology from the University of Pennsylvania. He has carried out original research in archaeology in Guatemala and Vermont, ethnography in Maine and Vermont and physical anthropology in Guatemala. This work has been the basis of over one hundred publications in various national and international books and journals, as well as in media intended for the general public.

His books include three widely used anthropology textbooks, as well as *The Original Vermonters*, co-authored with Marjory Power, and a technical monograph on ancient Maya settlement. He also served as consultant for the award-winning telecourse *Faces of Culture*. Besides his teaching and writing, Dr. Haviland has lectured to numerous professional, as well as nonprofessional, audiences in Canada, Mexico, Lesotho, South Africa and Spain, as well as in the United States.

A staunch supporter of indigenous rights, he served as expert witness for the Missisquoi Abenakis of Vermont in an important court case over aboriginal fishing rights. Awards received by Dr. Haviland include being named University Scholar by the graduate school of the University of Vermont in 1990; a Certificate of Appreciation from the Sovereign Republic of the Abenaki Nation of the Missisquoi, St. Francis/Sokoki Band in 1996; and a Lifetime Achievement Award from the Center for Research on Vermont in 2006.

ABOUT THE AUTHOR

William A. Haviland (left) with Penobscot elder Charles Norman Shay (right). The basket was purchased by Haviland in the mid-1950s from Charles's parents. Returned to Charles in 2005, it now is included in his family museum, Princess Watawaso's Tepee, on Indian Island, Maine.

Now retired from teaching, Haviland continues his research, writing and lecturing from the coast of Maine. His most recent book is *At the Place of the Lobsters and Crabs* (2009). In addition, he has served as president of the Island Heritage Trust on Deer Isle and presently serves on the boards of the Deer Isle–Stonington Historical Society and the Abbe Museum in Bar Harbor, where he holds the title of secretary of the corporation.

www.ingramcontent.com/pod-product-compliance
Lightning Source LLC
Chambersburg PA
CBHW060808100426
42813CB00004B/988